C.1

346
Englebardt, Leland S.
    You Have a Right.

DATE DUE

APR 1 0 1987			
DEC 1 6 1988			

*You Have
a Right*

You Have a Right

A Guide for Minors

Leland S. Englebardt

LOTHROP, LEE & SHEPARD COMPANY

A Division of William Morrow & Co., Inc.
New York

Library of Congress Cataloging in Publication Data
Englebardt, Leland S.
   You have a right.
   SUMMARY: Discusses the often misunderstood legal rights of young people
and gives information about where to go for help.
   1. Children—Legal status, laws, etc.—United States—Juvenile literature.
[1. Law. 2. Children's rights] I. Title.
KF479.Z9E53   346'.73'013   79-4678
ISBN 0-688-41893-7   ISBN 0-688-51893-1 lib. bdg.

This book is dedicated to my parents,

Stanley and Rita

Acknowledgments

No book, especially one attempting to explain the law, can get very far without the advice of a great many people whose experience and knowledge in special fields far exceeds the author's. To a few of these generous people I must extend thanks: Paula Gold of the Massachusetts Attorney General's Office; William R. Baird of the Bill Baird Center, Hempstead, N.Y. and Boston, Mass.; Howard Davidson of Greater Boston Legal Services; and Professor Robert Bloom of Boston College Law School.

Just as important as those who spoke to me were the friends who listened to my rough drafts and judged what they heard. For remaining on speaking terms through the many days of rewriting and nights of typing, my gratitude goes to Billy DeBear, Joyce Masters, Fred Rom, Ellen Saftler, and Lynn Englebardt.

Contents

1
The Law Belongs to You

Millions of Americans, minors included, are virtually ignorant of their legal and constitutional rights. They take no
care to protect them. Yet they are shocked when they find
themselves cheated or involved in a court struggle. Very
often, their unhappiness could have been avoided if they had
paused to ask themselves the basic question: Do I have a
right which I can protect?

Could it happen to you? Yes. Consider the following
examples:

Greg, Jeff, and David, all sixteen years old, have pooled
their limited financial resources in order to spend the summer at Lake Champlain. The three strike a bargain with a
man named O'Henry, owner of a dozen lakeside cottages,

to occupy a dilapidated house from June through August at only one hundred dollars a month—one fifth the normal rent. In return, the boys agree to make a variety of repairs before the end of the summer: replacing rotting floorboards and shingles, repainting, and clearing weeds from around the house.

On June 27, when O'Henry comes to collect the second month's rent, he sees that the boys have nearly completed the agreed-upon repairs. The appearance of the cottage is considerably improved. O'Henry realizes that once repainting is completed, he will be able to rent it at a much higher rate. After accepting their money, he tells the boys that he's had a better offer for the cottage. They must move out by the end of the month.

"Hey, what about our deal?" Greg protests.

"Sorry kids," O'Henry responds, "but you're all under age. Your signature on a lease doesn't mean a thing."

Despite their pleading, O'Henry refuses to budge from his decision. So, dejectedly, the boys pack their bags and go home.

Myron, seventeen years old, is "hanging out" with five friends in the parking lot of their suburban high school during lunch period. One of the boys gets a can of beer from his car, although he is under the legal drinking age, and three of the group take swigs from it. *Myron does not.* A few minutes later the boys split up to return to classes.

Two days later Myron is called to the principal's office where a staff secretary reads him a letter which says that "a member of the faculty" observed him "drinking beer in the parking lot." As a result, she says, Myron and his friends are suspended from school for a week, and "the principal does not wish to discuss the matter any further."

Steve and Kathy are on a backpacking trip on the Appalachian Trail when they are caught in a thunderstorm. Seeking shelter from the downpour, they spot an abandoned farmhouse several yards to the west and make a run for it. They arrive soaking wet, only to find the front door nailed shut, with a faded sign reading "No Trespassing—Property of M. Thompson."

Farther down the sagging front porch, however, is an open window. Steve peers in. "I can't see a thing," he tells Kathy. "It's too dark. But at least it's dry."

"That's good enough for me," Kathy replies. "I guess we won't disturb the ghosts if we make ourselves at home until the rain stops."

Steve drops his pack and swings a leg in over the rotting windowsill. Suddenly there is a sharp snap; Steve cries out in pain and falls forward into the house. Kathy grabs a flashlight from her pack and shines it inside. She sees Steve lying on the floor, his left foot caught in a large spring trap, the leg of his jeans already stained with blood. The device apparently had been placed there by Thompson to catch trespassers.

Kathy spots the lights of the Thompson house across a field. "I'm going for help," she tells Steve. When she arrives, though, her plea for aid gets an unfriendly reception.

"You kids got what you deserve for breaking into other people's houses," Thompson says. "Now get off my property before I call the police."

Frightened by Thompson's attitude, Kathy runs back to

Steve. Together they pry the trap off his ankle, which she bandages as best she can with surgical tape and gauze from their first-aid kit. Wearing her own pack and dragging Steve's with her free hand, Kathy helps him limp out of the house to a main road. They hitch a ride to the nearest clinic. When the doctor asks them how Steve came by his injury, they say he stepped on a trap in the woods. They make no mention of Thompson.

The teen-agers in these three situations are not simply the victims of bad luck, and they have much more in common than just resentment against the adults who took advantage of them. In one way or another, they all have been cheated of their legal or constitutional rights by people acting out of greed, hostility, or ignorance. To make matters worse, these teen-agers seem unaware that they have any legal rights at all. Some young people, in fact, would be convinced under these circumstances that they were the greater wrongdoers and were fortunate to escape further punishment.

Most of us are familiar with the kind of law violations that make colorful newspaper headlines: bank holdups, drug dealing, terrorist bombing, hijacking, and other criminal acts. The policemen and "private eyes" we see in television programs spend their time tracking down murderers, pushers, and terrorists. All these people are in trouble because they've broken the criminal law—a system of statutes (rules written and enacted by federal, state, or local legislatures) that provide for imprisonment as a punishment for those who break them.

There is another kind of law, however, which may not be as exciting or as often in the headlines as the criminal law, but which is just as important. This is the civil law—most simply defined as a system of regulations that governs the interaction of individuals, businesses, and governmental bodies. It includes not only statutes, but past decisions of courts of law, the written legal opinions of learned authorities, and even habits or customs peculiar to different parts of the country. Its source may be anything from a decision made last week in a country courthouse to the rights set down in the United States Constitution. In fact, this is where we get the phrase "civil rights"—a term which means that all people, no matter what their age, are entitled to enjoy the freedoms granted by the Constitution.

Whether we realize it or not, all of us spend a vast majority of our lives dealing with the civil law. It doesn't always confront us directly, as when we see red lights at intersections, "No Smoking" signs in public places, or a cruising police car. But it is present when we buy or rent a car or house, when we voice our opinions to others, and even when we choose the route home from school or work. For example, it certainly isn't a crime to take a shortcut by walking across a neighbor's yard, even if you crawl through a hole in his fence to do it. But you are trespassing —in legal terms, when you enter on your neighbor's land without his permission you are violating his right of privacy. If your neighbor complains to you or demands that you stop using the shortcut, he is enforcing his rights the same way a policeman enforces the criminal law. You must not use his land.

In civil law, the rights of one person are always being balanced, or weighed, against the rights of another person or group of people. In the example just given, your right to walk where you please is being compared to your neighbor's

15

right to have his property undisturbed. These sorts of rights are never absolute. This means that the rights of both parties will not remain the same under all circumstances. If you were being chased by a vicious dog and ran across another person's property to escape, your immediate need to avoid injury from the dog would outweigh the other party's right of privacy.

As part of the "balancing act" by which we decide who is privileged to act in a certain way and who is not, some types of individuals receive special consideration under the law. Minors—persons under eighteen years of age—are among the most important of these special classes.

The issue of minors' rights—their powers to do what they want within the law—is prominent nationwide. Never before in history have young people been so numerous, possessed with such mobility and buying power, and enjoyed so many legal rights and privileges.

Minors' rights received their first major boost in 1937 when the U.S. Supreme Court (the highest court in the land and the final word on American law) upheld a Washington statute which established a minimum wage for women and minors. In its opinion, the Court called these two groups "a class of workers who are in an unequal position with respect to bargaining power and are thus defenseless against denial of a living wage . . ." These words signaled the beginning of national recognition that minors are entitled to special legal consideration to make up for their lack of social influence and political power.

The Supreme Court's decision—and the many laws and judicial decisions that followed it—came just in time for a social revolution which greatly changed the role of young people in our country. For one thing, the under-eighteen

16

population has more than doubled since the Court wrote its words over forty years ago. At that time, most children were expected to seek work as soon as they were strong enough. They were *not* expected to have any political opinions. Today, children are encouraged to pursue higher education; over sixty percent go on to college. They have a greater voice within the family. And, with the advent of the eighteen-year-old vote, more attention is being paid by elected officials to the political viewpoints of this group.

Yet, along with increased freedoms, the newfound buying power and influence of people under eighteen have created problems. These problems grow in complexity every day as new laws are passed, and as state and federal courts interpret existing laws.

One example: we recognize that very young children may lack the judgment to be responsible for their own actions. But at what age does a child develop adequate reasoning? Should we simply establish a fixed age that applies to all children, or must we consider each individual case? What tests do we use to measure judgment? These are just a few of the many questions that face lawyers, judges, and lawmakers today.

Another kind of problem is the growing wave of juvenile crime and violence that has brought ever increasing numbers of young people into direct involvement with the law and law enforcement agencies. Statistics in this area are often staggering. *Violent Delinquents*, a Ford Foundation study released in 1978, stated that the number of juveniles arrested for violent crimes—homicide, rape, robbery, and assault—had shot up over three hundred percent in the preceding fifteen years.

Evidence collected by the U.S. Senate Judiciary Sub-

17

committee on Juvenile Delinquency shows that during the period between 1970 and 1973, assaults on primary and secondary school students by their classmates increased eighty-five percent. Assaults on teachers by students went up seventy-seven percent during the same period. According to testimony given at Subcommittee hearings, the cost to school systems of student vandalism, arson, and theft runs to half a billion dollars a year. Preserving the special, individual rights of minors while trying to halt this violence and destruction is a major problem in the legal community.

Some public school systems have responded to the problems of delinquency and ignorance of fundamental rights by offering programs of legal education designed specifically for minors. According to a 1976 report in *Juris Doctor*, a lawyers' magazine, the number of law-related courses has increased from a 1971 total of 100 in six states to over 400 programs in thirty states.

But as impressive as these figures seem, the American Bar Association's Special Committee on Youth Education for Citizenship has found that the programs reach less than five percent of the nation's fifty million students.

Besides reaching only a small number of students, such courses often miss the point. Because the teachers who conduct them have a background in government or history, they tend to overemphasize those areas. While it's good to know that some elements of our legal system have roots as far back as the Norman Conquest of England in 1066, or that the executive and legislative branches of government interact to create law, some more practical information is needed. All too often the more immediate questions of how a minor may safeguard his or her rights when confronted by a landlord, employer, or policeman are neglected.

Greg, Jeff, and David, our three friends by the lake, would certainly have fared better if they had known about their contract rights. O'Henry's claim that their signatures were meaningless is without basis. On the contrary, any contract signed by a minor—whether to buy an automobile, lease a house, or for any purpose except purchasing real estate—is presumed to be valid.

Unfortunately, by packing up and going home the boys gave up their rights, as well as the time, money, and effort they had put into fulfilling their part of the bargain. They had every legal right to stay and enjoy a great summer.

By the same token, Myron and his beer-drinking friends stand to lose a great deal more than just a summer's fun if they don't enforce their rights. A suspension usually becomes part of a student's permanent academic record and may someday become a block to college admission or a good job. But some students are reluctant to protest what they feel is unjust because they assume that the principal's word is law, or that the school administration is somehow beyond the law. This is simply false. Though it may be an overused phrase, it is still true that "all persons are equal under the law"—and this includes students in their dealings with school officials.

In this case, the principal didn't give Myron a chance to tell his version of the story, or to defend himself in any way against the charge of drinking beer. Under the law of the land, this is a violation of Myron's constitutional right of "due process of law," for the U.S. Constitution guarantees all of us, no matter what age, an opportunity to be heard in our own defense.

Steve and Kathy, the unfortunate backpackers, didn't lose their rights because they were denied an opportunity

19

to explain their actions; they cheated themselves by not taking advantage of a chance that was offered to them. Had they told the truth when the doctor asked Steve how he got his injury, they might have learned that booby-trapping your land or home is a much greater wrong than harmless trespassing.

Here we can see the "balancing act" of rights, which we discussed earlier, taking place. Clearly Steve and Kathy were in the wrong when they entered the house, because they infringed on Thompson's right of privacy. However, the force that the landowner used to secure his right was unreasonable. The trap was put in a position where it could cause great injury to anyone coming into the house. It is simple common sense, as well as the law, that the right to life is superior to that of property. One of the most importent texts in modern law practice, the *Restatement of Torts*, states that "a possessor of land has no privilege to use force . . . to cause death or serious harm against another whom the possessor sees about to enter his premises . . . unless the intrusion threatens death or serious bodily harm to the occupiers or users of the premises." In other words, the only time you are legally permitted to use a weapon is in defense of your own life.

Taking into account the relative wrongs committed by both parties, we can see that the balance of rights weighs heavily on Steve's side. "Serious bodily harm" was done to him by Thompson's act of setting the trap, while his own act of trespassing endangered neither lives nor property. In both the real and legal sense, Steve is the only injured party. But ignorance of his rights precluded court action that would have compensated him for his injuries.

It seems that almost everything we do somehow involves

the law. But does this mean that you should go running to a lawyer every time you have a disagreement? Some people might say yes. In America, lawsuits have been an increasingly popular method of resolving disputes. In 1975 alone, over four million legal battles were started in U.S. courts.

Don't forget, though, that it is often easier—and always safer—to avoid a situation that leads to conflict than to take it to court. This is where awareness of your rights can enable you to prevent disagreements which might otherwise lead to the expense and frustration of a lawsuit. No sensible person would call for professional advice every time he or she stepped onto someone else's property, or purchased something in a store, or did anything else that changed his or her legal relationship with others. Knowing your rights can keep you out of trouble; consultation with a lawyer usually comes only after a problem has arisen.

2
History's Children

Recently a sixteen-year-old friend of mine purchased a used car. It was an event he had looked forward to for a long time. He had worked part-time in a local restaurant to earn the money and had even attended a course in auto mechanics at our community college the previous summer. In fact, when I came over to look at his new wheels at least half the engine was spread around the garage on pieces of newspaper, waiting to be cleaned and reassembled.

"It's a real mean machine," he told me with pride. "Ended up costing a little more than I'd planned to spend. My dad wanted me to forget about a car and save the money, but I'm the one who worked for it so I bought what I wanted with it."

Today, in the final quarter of the twentieth century, many young people take statements and actions like these for granted. They hardly think it unusual to be able to attend school and hold an afternoon job at the same time, or to make their own decisions about how to spend the money they earn. Yet these are privileges which have been generally recognized as belonging to minors only in recent years. If we examine the history of minors' rights in America it is easy to see that the position of young people in today's society is a far cry from the attitude toward children that was brought to our shores hundreds of years ago by the first English settlers.

In fact, many of the first children to arrive in the American colonies were bought and sold much the same as slaves. They were orphans and children of the poor from overcrowded English slums. Purchased from public workhouses (orphanages run by the city) or in some cases shanghaied by agents of shipping companies, they were transported to the colonies to become indentured servants, laborers, and apprentices. Starting at the age of ten or twelve or even younger, they were bound by contract to a master until they reached twenty-one. Few laws governed the conditions of their service. Boys unlucky enough to be put in the care of a cruel master could look forward to years of beatings, hard labor, and bare survival.

Children who remained with their natural families may have received kinder treatment, but they lived under an equally strict code of conduct. Life for most people in the early settlements was a constant battle against the wilderness and the elements. Boys began accompanying their fathers to the fields or the shop as soon as they were physically able. Girls were taught the "womanly" tasks of cooking and clothes-making at a tender age. Although the New England colonies began requiring the public maintenance of schoolmasters in most towns as early as 1647, school attendance was not compulsory. Many young people therefore knew only what ABC's their parents had time to teach them.

In the colonial home the Bible was the first source of wisdom in child-rearing. Parents were reminded again and again by clergymen and public officials, "He that spareth the rod hateth his son, but he that loveth him chasteneth him betimes." So from an early age most children were accustomed to receiving regular whippings whether they misbehaved or not.

For those who did oppose their parents' wishes, however, far more serious punishments lay in store. In 1646 the colony of Massachusetts provided the death penalty for any child over sixteen who "shall curse or smite their natural father or mother." Four years later Connecticut passed a similar law. It is doubtful that any children were actually put to death under those laws, but many judges ordered public lashings for disrespectful youngsters.

Young people had no voice in the running of the early American household. The word of an elder was never to be questioned. "Never sit in the presence of thy parents without bidding, tho' no stranger be present," commanded a book on children's etiquette printed in 1715. "If thou passest by thy parents, and any place where thou seest them, bow towards them. Never speak to thy parents without some title of respect—Sir, Madam, etc. Beware thou utter not any thing hard to be believed."

The American Revolution did much to disrupt those traditions. As with most wars, it was fought mainly by young people. But also, many leaders of the rebellion were young: General Henry Knox was only twenty-six in 1776, future President James Madison was twenty-five in that year, and Alexander Hamilton, later to become the first Secretary of the Treasury, was twenty-one.

In questioning the policies of their king and "mother country," American youths learned that even the most respected of institutions might be wrong. Once they had turned away from that time-honored government, it was only natural that they would begin to re-examine the wisdom of other figures of authority closer to home. Eventually they would come to doubt their parents and superiors in the community.

Another important force that worked against the traditional family unit was the arrival of the industrial age. The first mechanized cotton mills were established in New England during the latter part of the eighteenth century. These early "manufactories" bore little resemblance to the sprawling industrial plants that we see across America today. The mills were housed in narrow, red-brick buildings on winding streets. The rooms where workers tended the spindles, combs, and bobbins of the weaving machines were usually small, dimly lighted, and poorly ventilated. Ten- and twelve-hour working days were common, and the mill was in operation six days a week.

Factory employment broke down the traditionally superior position of parents in the family. Instead of being his own boss in his shop or on the farm, the father was as much a subject of the factory foreman as the child was. Now the child's instruction in the skills of his trade was handled not by a concerned parent but by a supervisor who had many other children under his command.

25

From the beginning, children were favored as mill employees because of their dexterity—"small, quick fingers were admirably suited for picking up and knotting broken threads," wrote one historian—and the minimal wages they earned. A mill worker age ten or younger often was paid less than fifty cents a week.

Working conditions in many mills around 1790 were very much like the apprenticeships which had been common in America for years. Workers of eight or ten were taught by foremen and mill operators, and occasionally became quite skilled at production or at fixing machinery.

During the nineteenth century the total population increased over fourteen times. Factories did the work once handled by individual craftsmen. Almost every process could be done faster and more cheaply by machines.

As demand grew, factory owners employed more young people; by 1900, 700,000 children under age of sixteen were employed in industrial production nationwide.

Despite this demand for their services, working children in the early nineteenth century had no more legal rights than their ancestors had had on the farm. They had no control over the money they earned, which in most cases was paid directly to their parents. They couldn't sign a contract. Parents in need of money could advertise their children for sale in public newspapers. Parents and employers could abuse their young charges through beating or overwork almost to the point of death without fear of legal interference.

Josiah Quincy, later to become mayor of Boston and president of Harvard University, was among the first to draw public attention to the plight of the factory child.

"Pity those little creatures," he wrote after visiting a mill in 1801, "plying in a contracted room, among flyers and cogs, at an age when nature requires for them air, space and sports. There is a dull dejection in the countenance of all of them."

It would be years before the pleas of Quincy and others like him would arouse state legislatures to take steps toward protecting working children. The first law regulating child labor was passed in Connecticut in 1813. It required mill and factory operators to provide some sort of education for children in their employ. By 1860 all the New England states had passed similar laws. But at best these rules required only a few months of schooling each year and it is not known how many manufacturers obeyed. In 1870 it was reported that only fifty-seven percent of all American children between the ages of five and seventeen were attending school.

Around mid-century the lawmakers began to look more closely at actual conditions inside the factory and the home. An Illinois court took the first step when it handed down a landmark decision on the limits of a parent's power to punish a child. After hearing the case of Sam Fletcher, a blind boy who was locked in the unheated cellar of his home by his father and stepmother for several winter days and allowed to become filthy and covered with insects, the court said "children must (not) be left, without the protection of the law, at the mercy of depraved men or women, with the liberty to inflict any species of barbarity short of actual taking of life."

In the years that followed, more courts began to draw a line between proper punishment and brutality. Societies for Prevention of Cruelty to Children were founded across the nation. The abused child finally had someplace to turn for help.

Yet with each law that was passed to help poor and working children, social reformers uncovered still more horrible conditions. In New York City, illegally employed children were found imprisoned in a cellar and never allowed to go outside. In Paterson, New Jersey, thirteen-year-old girls worked all day in a steam-filled flax mill twisting coils of wet hemp, only to have to walk home dripping wet in winter and summer. In the mines of West Virginia, nine- and ten-year-old "breaker boys" were paid sixty cents a day to crouch over coal chutes for ten hours at a time, hand-picking rocks from the moving stream.

The harmful effects of these occupations did not stop at the factory gate. Kids who inhaled the thick dust of the mills, mines, or furniture factories often developed crippling lung diseases. Breaker boys became stooped and round-shouldered from the long hours of bending over the chutes. Youngsters whose skins were stained with poison from working in dye factories sometimes died from a minor cut.

The wide circulation of these facts in the years after the Civil War prompted lawmakers to step up their efforts to improve the lot of the working child. State after state passed regulations prohibiting the employment of very young children in manufacturing. Requirements that working children receive an adequate education were stiffened, and for the first time employers were made legally responsible for maintaining safe working conditions. By degrees, the maximum number of hours in a child's working week was shortened from sixty to forty-eight or even less.

But the ground gained by reformers was not always held for long. In Alabama, reports of "little children of six and seven years who were at work for twelve or thirteen hours a day in cotton mills" pushed the legislature to enact an eight-hour limit for workers under fourteen. In 1894, only seven years after the law was passed, cotton industry forces succeeded in having it repealed.

Private organizations soon joined the battle against child labor. Union leader Samuel Gompers described seeing children "six and seven and eight years of age, seated in the middle of a room on the floor, in all the dirt and dust, stripping tobacco. Shame upon such crimes," he thundered in conclusion, "and shame upon us if we do not raise our voices against them." In 1894, with Gompers as its president, the newly formed American Federation of Labor endorsed an eight-hour day for women and children.

While these actions began to have the effect of taking young people out of factories, other laws began pushing them into schoolrooms. In 1918 Mississippi became the last state to make education compulsory. This meant that the factory inspectors and truant officers in all states had the power to remove an underage worker from his job and, in some cases, to levy a fine on his employer for breaking the law.

While a great many people were working to emancipate children from "the harsh, pitiless authority of an employer," others were trying to help youngsters who rebelled against the system and wound up in jail. Traditionally, minors who broke the law were charged with a crime, tried in public court and, if convicted, were sent to the same prisons as adults. This led to punishments which seem far too severe today—in the early 1900s a child of thirteen received the death penalty for murder and an eight-year-old was executed for arson.

Conditions in prisons, especially those for minorities in the South, were unbelievably bad. "Men are there chained with their necks in an iron collar and joined to ankle chains," reported a minister who visited a South Carolina jail in 1880. "A young boy of fourteen wears hand cuffs and the irons have cut into his wrists. The beds are rotten straw, full of vermin."

By the end of the nineteenth century, however, many states were adopting the idea that young people would be better off in institutions designed not simply to punish, but to train them for a productive life in society. Different states experimented with different methods. Massachusetts, New York, and California tried placing young men on ships, where professional officers trained them in seamanship. But the floating reform schools were stopped in the years after the Civil War because of their high operating expenses and because of economic depressions which almost eliminated the commercial demand for sailors.

Farm schools proliferated in the northern states. In these, it was believed, hard work and fresh air would turn troublesome children to a life of goodness. Unfortunately, the farm schools were rarely able to bring in enough money by selling their products. To fill in the gap, the practice of "contract labor" was begun with local businessmen. Under the contract labor system the youngsters were put into the custody of a factory or farm in the area every day and forced to work. Naturally they never saw the money that they earned. Moreover, floggings and other forms of physical punishment were routinely delivered by the foremen who had absolute power during working hours.

Back inside the reform school at night, without any chance to show their resentment toward the factory owners or the state officials who guarded them, the children turned on each other. Riots and fires broke out in the dormitories. Beatings were common and sometimes boys were simply found in the morning murdered in their beds.

As early as 1875, social critics began objecting to the reform school system. Some attacked the idea that a large institution with hundreds of inmates could teach proper values. Others decried the practice of contract labor, which made the boys virtual slaves of the state.

In 1884 New York responded to these arguments by abandoning its contract labor system. In several states charitable organizations were able to obtain state backing to open private reformatories where children received more personal attention and instruction. But problems of cost, violence, and the simple fact that few young offenders were actually "reformed" by their stay continued to plague such schools.

Meanwhile, judges and lawmakers across the nation were at work on a new, special set of rules to apply to kids who were brought into court. The goal of those who wrote these new rules was to protect youngsters in trouble by keeping them separate from older criminals. To do this, the reformers created the juvenile court. This special court, which is still in use today, is devoted solely to hearing cases against young people.

Unlike the formal trials in criminal courts, which involve lawyers and witnesses and are open to the public, a hearing in juvenile court was made private. Only the judge, the child, often the parent, and a court official met in a small room to discuss the case. Instead of being pronounced guilty or innocent after the hearing, the child was judged to be "delinquent" or "not delinquent." This was more than just a change in wording: it meant that in the eyes of the law no crime had been committed. Therefore the young offender was not to be punished but guided back to a "normal relation to society," a law-abiding life.

A major part of the new juvenile court system was the practice of allowing most youngsters judged "delinquent" to remain with their families. No matter how bad the family situation was, the alternative of being locked up in prison or reform school was worse. While at home, the child was visited regularly by an older person whose job was to keep him from breaking the law again. In this arrangement, known as "probation," the juvenile court tried to make use of the home and its natural parental authority to teach the child how to live within the law.

Yet, the hopeful vision of probation as a "reformatory without walls" rarely came true in America's city streets. In some cases the probation officers who visited the delinquents at home were poorly trained, or too few in number to provide adequate supervision. Many lawmakers became concerned that without the formalities of a trial by jury there was no way to make sure that a judge was being fair in his decision. Even judges themselves were critical of their courts, which one described as being "in a perpetual state of semi-starvation, understaffed, underpaid and ill-housed."

As the years passed it was seen that the unique rules of juvenile court, while much more fair than the old system, were not the cure-all that some had hoped. In 1950, author Albert Deutsch reported visiting an Indiana reform school where boys were lashed with a leather whip for laziness, possessing tobacco, or using vulgar language. As recently as 1970, beating and solitary confinement were reported in a North Carolina "training school" for delinquent children. Today it is estimated that half a million young people are under state care outside their homes and thousands of them are subjected to cruelty, overcrowding, and filthy conditions.

The fault, however, does not lie totally within the juvenile justice system. One major reason for the inadequate remedies of juvenile courts and the poor record of reform schools is the skyrocketing rate of youth crime. In July, 1977, *Time* magazine reported that "more than half of all serious crimes in the U.S. are committed by youths aged ten to seventeen. Since 1960, juvenile crime has risen twice as fast as that of adults."

While most people think of shoplifting and petty vandalism when they hear the words "juvenile delinquent," the frightening truth is that children as young as six years old are being arrested for robbery, assault, and murder in staggering numbers.

There are many reasons for this surge of violent crime, but prominent among them is a disdain for the procedures of the juvenile court. The rules designed to treat youngsters gently and give them a chance to avoid criminal records are used as a "free out" by troublemakers. "Who cares about getting caught," say young toughs arrested for rape or carrying a loaded gun, "when the worst that can happen to me is a few months in reform school? I'll probably just get sent home. It's all a big joke."

Across the courtroom, however, no one is laughing. In fact, many judges and lawyers are now working to reverse the soft treatment that has been the hallmark of juvenile court. In cities from New York to New Orleans a kid brought to court for any violent crime has a greater chance of winding up in prison today than he did five years ago. Whereas in 1900 it could be said that the main purpose of juvenile court was to "protect neglected childhood," in 1978 more people might have agreed with Memphis juvenile court judge Kenneth Turner: "Rather than simply emphasize the needs of the child, we also figure we have a paramount duty to protect society."

Whether this stiffer attitude toward delinquents will reduce the soaring amount of youth crime and whether it signals a major change in the role of the court are questions that can't yet be answered. But it is clear that a teen-age mugger or burglar can no longer be confident of returning to the streets within a few days or weeks after his hearing.

At about the same time that the states were setting up juvenile courts, the federal government was becoming deeply involved in the area of children's rights. In 1906 President Theodore Roosevelt called for "a drastic and thoroughgoing child labor law." Four years later he hosted advocates from across the nation at the First White House Conference on Care of Dependent Children.

One result of this talk was the Sheppard-Towner Act, a law providing money to the states "for the promotion of the welfare and hygiene of maternity and infancy." In 1935 federal child care assistance was expanded to include aid to crippled, homeless, and neglected children. This new flow of money, which has continued through the present day, has been directly responsible for the virtual elimination of diseases such as smallpox, cholera, and polio, which once killed thousands of children every year.

The federal aid has also created legal rights. Children in

states that receive funds from Washington have a legal right to the health services which that money is supposed to provide. Non-profit legal groups now exist in most major cities to assist young people who feel they have been denied proper medical care under a public program. This combination of affirmative government programs and independent watchdog agencies has created a growing body of laws which seek to give all children the most basic requirement of a productive life: good health.

But while most of the legal battles over childrens' medical care have taken place behind the scenes, arguments in another area of the law have hogged the headlines and caused bitter fighting in the streets of American cities. Education, especially the right of minorities to an equal seat in the classroom, has proved to be one of the most explosive legal issues of the twentieth century.

None would dispute President John F. Kennedy's statement that "the doors to the schoolhouse, to the library and to the college lead to the richest treasures of our society." Yet, since the 1930s few have agreed on how those doors should be opened or who should pass through them.

Schools across the nation found themselves in trouble when the economic pressures of the Great Depression left them with no money to pay teachers or buy books. They turned to the federal government for assistance. In response, Congress authorized grants to keep schools open and loans up to $75,000,000 to meet teachers' paychecks.

Because they were spending such large amounts on education, federal officials were naturally concerned that the taxpayers' money be distributed fairly among all groups in need. Studies revealed, however, that in countless cases the funds were detoured away from black children, who as late as the 1950s were still forced by state laws to attend schools separate from those of whites.

Differences between black and white educational quality were painfully obvious. Said a white truant officer in Shelby County, Tennessee, "It just isn't safe for me to go on a plantation to bring students to school. The landowners tell me to let the niggers work." These words might have been spoken in the age of slavery, but the year was 1941.

In that same year sociologist Charles Johnson reported visiting a rural school for blacks in "a dilapidated building, with broken benches inside that are crowded to three times their normal capacity. Only a few battered books are in sight, and we look in vain for maps or charts." Teachers for the all-black schools, Johnson wrote, were appointed "in a most casual manner" by whites. A woman who had been a good housekeeper or nursemaid was often made a teacher without any regard for her knowledge or ability to communicate.

In a series of important decisions from 1938 to 1950, the U.S. Supreme Court began to chip away at the legal walls that surrounded minority children. The Court declared that the fourteenth amendment to the Constitution, which requires the states to guarantee to all people "equal protection of the laws," prohibited the state governments from passing a special law for people of a different race or color. Because of this constitutional requirement, a black youth could not be kept out of a graduate school on grounds of his race and it was illegal to make minority students sit at separate tables or desks marked "For Colored Only."

The end of racial barriers under the law was finally made clear in 1954 by the Supreme Court's famous decision in the case of *Brown v. Board of Education of Topeka.*

"We conclude," wrote Chief Justice Earl Warren, "that in the field of public education the doctrine of 'separate but equal' has no place. Separate educational facilities are inherently unequal." With these words the Court brought about the end of all state laws that kept white children in one schoolhouse and blacks in another.

The *Brown* decision unleashed a storm of controversy and resistance to integration that has not subsided to this day. The first major confrontation occurred at Central High School in Little Rock, Arkansas, where the attendance of only eight black students sparked organized resistance and mob violence by whites. The situation became so serious that President Eisenhower took to radio and TV to announce that Army troops would be sent to the city to enforce integration.

This racial hatred did not stop in Little Rock. In Holmes County, Mississippi, the white community responded to a court order to mix the races with a boycott of the public school system. In Surry County, Virginia, every white student and teacher left the schools when seven black children were brought in. And in Boston, Massachusetts, racist crowds blocked buses carrying young people to integrated schools and attacked any black person they could find. "Even now," said one Boston lawyer in 1978, "when a black family goes to a parent-teacher conference in some neighborhoods we have to take them in a police car for their own safety."

Racial conflict wasn't the only legal problem in American schools. In the 1960s long hair and outlandish dress replaced the crew cut and football jacket as the symbols of modern kids. Teen-agers used marijuana to "turn on" instead of beer. And a war in the faraway nation of Vietnam was causing young people to question their government in the same way their great-great-great-grandfathers had doubted the English king before the Revolutionary War.

The clash between students and school officials over the right to speak out against the government or to wear unusual clothing produced many court cases. In Iowa, three students who were suspended from school for wearing black armbands in class to protest the Vietnam war went to court for help. Their case went all the way to the Supreme Court, which decided that wearing the armbands was a way of voicing their political opinion and was therefore protected by the Constitution. A Wisconsin boy suspended for wearing long hair also went to the Court, which declared his punishment illegal.

In these cases as well as others, the Court has stressed the modern belief that young people are entitled to as many rights under the Constitution as their elders. "Students in school as well as out of school," wrote Justice Abe Fortas, "are possessed of fundamental rights which the states must respect." This was certainly a long way from the days when a child could be bought and sold or made to work for a term of years like a slave.

In the 1970s these rights have been extended by courts and legislatures to include children with special problems. Cases in New York, Michigan, Pennsylvania and other states have established the right of mentally retarded and emotionally handicapped children to receive a free public education just as any other citizen can. And federal law now requires equality for the *physically* handicapped. But conflict and doubt continue over who has the final authority to decide what is best for those youngsters. The clash is often between a state welfare agency and the parents of a handicapped boy or girl. Situations where a parent wants to withdraw a "special child" from school or even allow him to die by denying permission for needed surgery present difficult decisions for judges.

The changes now taking place in youth law are the result of a trend toward seeing the child more as an individual and an equal under the law. No longer are kids regarded as possessions of their parents, to be used or ignored as the family sees fit. They can work on their own and, to a great extent, make their own decisions.

With these rights have come increased responsibilities, such as curbing your right of free speech when it interferes with another person's right to learn in the classroom. This is part of the ever expanding role that young people play in modern society. While you may not give this role much thought as you attend school or work or buy your first car, you should be aware of the complex web of legal rights that allows you to do these things.

3
When You Sign on the Dotted Line

Made any contracts lately?

Most of us would immediately respond "no." That's because we usually think of a contract in only one way: as a piece of paper covered with complex legal writing, usually in microscopic print. To complete it, both parties must sign each other's copy in the presence of a witness, who must also sign.

Some contracts really are made this way. But far more involve no elaborate documents or ceremonies. Most contracts are created by simple things we do every day, such as going to the store or to our jobs. In fact, the law says that any time you spend money or do some work for another person you're forming some kind of contract. It doesn't require signing your name, or even a handshake.

When Billy decided to buy a motorbike, for example, he certainly didn't think of it as a contract. The shiny silver moped caught his eye as he passed the showroom window and that afternoon he paid three hundred dollars cash for it. When it was delivered the next day, Billy started it and imagined himself riding all over the county during the summer days ahead.

He hadn't gone more than five blocks, however, when his daydreams were interrupted by a blue light in his rearview mirror. "Where's your helmet, son?" the policeman asked after Billy had pulled to a stop. "Don't you know there's a local law against riding two-wheeled motorized vehicles without some head protection?"

"No," Billy admitted, "I didn't know that."

"Well, you'll have to have one next time. Let me see your permit number, so I can keep a record of it."

"What kind of permit do you mean?" Billy asked nervously.

"Don't tell me," the officer said, "that you also don't know you have to be sixteen and have a town permit to drive a moped in this county. How old are you?"

"Fifteen, sir."

"Then I guess there won't be a next time. You'd better get in the car." The policeman loaded the bike into the trunk of his cruiser and drove Billy home.

Billy's problem is obvious. He is now the owner of a moped that will be useless to him for another year. He used his whole savings to buy the bike and had hoped to make some spending money by using it to deliver packages. Now, however, that hope has been dashed and the coming summer looks bleak.

Luckily, Billy's older brother Richie came home from law school the next day. When Billy explained the situation Richie couldn't resist smiling. "You're not using your head, boy," he said. "You know that kids your age have special rights when they make a contract."

"We didn't sign any contract," Billy said sourly. "I just paid."

"That *is* a kind of contract," Richie corrected. "Just because you didn't sign anything doesn't mean you didn't make a deal. The agreement was that if you gave them money, they'd give you a bike. A contract, as pure and simple as they come. You both did what you agreed to do and the contract was complete."

"So now I'm stuck with it, right?"

"Wrong. A minor can get out of a contract if he makes a mistake. It sounds to me as if you made a pretty big one."

When a grown person makes a deal, Richie explained, he assumes full responsibility for his action. If the bargain is a bad one, the law will not prevent him from losing money or having to perform an unpleasant task—unless the deal is illegal.

But for young people it's a different story. The law recognizes that they are inexperienced in business transactions. Because of this, it's easy for a fast-talking salesman to take advantage. You may sign a contract you don't understand or spend more money than originally intended. Even if the salesman doesn't pressure you, you might buy something without thinking about it long enough. This was Billy's mistake.

To balance out this situation, a special rule was developed which gives you a second chance after making a deal. This rule is called "voidability." It means that as a minor (in most states, someone under eighteen years of age), you can cancel the contract. All you need to do is take back the item you bought or make it clear that you've changed your mind.

"Now," Richie went on, "because you're underage, returning what you got out of the bargain entitles you to get your money back. As long as the bike is still in new condition, they have to do it for you." When Richie took his brother and the moped back to the store, this is exactly what happened.

When you know that young people can void their contracts, the question naturally arises as to whether an older person has a similar privilege. After all, if one party has the right to cancel a deal, it seems only fair to allow the other side to do the same.

But if this were true the original purpose of the voidability rule would be lost. The law presumes that adults have enough experience in business not to need a second chance to think about their actions. Young people, on the other hand, are seen as easier prey for rip-off artists who use flashy sales techniques and promise something for nothing. This is a special rule that works in your favor.

As with every rule of law, however, voidability has a number of exceptions. One of these concerns a practice familiar to every American teen-ager. "Sure, I know I'm not the legal age to drink," says Harold, a fifteen-year-old from Texas. "But neither are my friends and they all do it. So when we go out to a bar, I use my older brother's I.D. card or I lie about my age. It's no big deal."

Everyone knows that underage drinking can lead to trouble with the police. But few are aware that in many states giving a false age when making a contract means forfeiting the right of voidability. This kind of lying can turn "no big deal" into a deal that you can't get out of.

Mary Beth found this out the hard way. With savings from a summer job she bought a small stereo system, paying the hi-fi store by check. Fearing that they wouldn't accept her check because she was underage, seventeen, she borrowed her twenty-year-old sister's driver's license to use for identification.

When she presented the card to the salesman, he looked it over carefully. "You're twenty, right?" he asked.

"Yes. But don't even look at the photo. It's so horrible I'm embarrassed to show it to people."

The salesman laughed and returned the license. "I know what you mean," he said. "Nobody's ever taken a good picture of me, either."

Mary Beth was pleased with her music system. But a week before she was due to leave for college, she was faced with a large and unexpected auto repair bill. Short of money, she thought she could return the record player, because it was still in new condition.

In this case, though, the deception had cost her the right to change her mind. "We still have the number from your driver's license," the manager said. "You claimed you were twenty, and you look about that age. In this state that means you aren't a minor and can't go back on the contract."

Of course, Mary Beth could have taken advantage of the store's normal exchange policy because that option is open to everyone. But voiding the contract and getting your money back is different from simply getting a credit slip good for something else in the same shop.

Another exception to the voidability rule is that you must always pay a debt which results from receiving "necessaries." What are "necessaries"? While there is no single definition of this term, it is generally recognized as anything you need to carry on a normal life and cannot get from any other source.

Obviously, food, clothing, and a place to sleep fall within this broad description. Courts have also said that a basic education is essential for every child in today's society. But in all other cases the facts must be examined to see whether the subject of the contract is really "necessary."

Such judgments are often quite difficult to make. For example, a private automobile would not ordinarily be considered indispensable to a seventeen-year-old. But this view might change if that young person were married and lived in a rural area where the car was his sole means of getting to work.

You can see how each new fact added to a situation can affect the decision. This means that the most important thing you can do to avoid possible legal hassles is to pause long enough to think of the *best* way to get what you need, not just the easiest way. Otherwise you might end up in court trying to prove that what you received wasn't a "necessary." Even worse, you could be forced to pay for something you already have.

You may be wondering what has happened to written contracts, the kind we mentioned at the beginning of this chapter. Such formal agreements are used almost exclusively in the business world. To those familiar with their special form and language, written contracts are a safe and practical way of making sure promises are kept.

But they can also be a trap for the unwary. Every year thousands of young people create problems for themselves by making bad deals. Whether you are victimized by a con man, fail to read what you are signing, or just don't understand the terms of the agreement, the result is trouble. You have created an obligation you can't fulfill.

Theresa made this mistake. At age fourteen she was a slim 5' 2" with flowing hair and dark brown eyes. These qualities allowed her to earn a little spending money by modeling for a family friend who designed children's clothes. Twice a week Theresa took the bus to the woman's studio where she was photographed and sketched wearing skirts, blouses, and bathing suits.

It was after one of the picture-taking sessions that Mark, a young man who worked in the studio, approached her. "I've noticed you around here," he said. "Need a ride home?"

Theresa was hesitant. "Well, I don't think so. The bus takes me right down to Market Street, near my house."

"That's my direction too," Mark said, smiling. "C'mon. I'll give you door-to-door service."

During the trip Mark told her stories about studios he'd worked in and the glamorous people there. "Professional models really rake it in," he said. "Sometimes forty or fifty dollars an hour. After that they get into TV, or movies— anything they want."

"How do they do it?" Theresa asked, thinking that fifty dollars was more than she made in a month.

"The secret is knowing the right people, or having a manager who does. Who's your manager?"

"Oh," Theresa said, "I don't have one. The designer is a friend of my mother's."

"That's too bad," Mark said, reaching for a cigarette. "A manager is the key if you want high-paying work. I used to manage a couple of girls in your line."

"Really?"

"Sure. I've been in this business for years. I've got connections at most of the big agencies. They know my name. Tell you what, I'll do you a favor and take a look around. Of course I can't promise anything. But I'll see what I can do."

"Well . . . thanks," Theresa said.

The next time she came to the studio, Mark walked up with a paper in his hand. "The first thing you have to do," he said, "is sign this. It just says that I'm officially trying to get work for you. Otherwise, you know, they might not believe that I really represent you."

Theresa looked at the page. It was covered with small print in numbered paragraphs and would have taken several minutes to read. But the silence as she scanned the first few sentences was already embarrassing her. Mark would think she didn't trust him.

"Where do I sign?" she asked, taking the pen he offered.

The following week Mark handed Theresa a small business card. "What did I tell you?" he said with an easy grin. "Get a manager like me and you're on the road. Just be at this address nine o'clock Thursday morning for a photo session."

Theresa was taken aback. "That's a school day. I have to be in class at that hour."

"Hey, listen," Mark said softly but firmly, "a model has to do what her manager tells her. That's part of the deal. So don't worry about skipping out on teacher. You just be at the studio."

That evening Theresa told her parents about the deal with Mark. Her father examined the business card and then went to the telephone. In a few minutes he was back.

"This guy Mark is a swindler," he said, throwing the card on the dining table. "That contract you signed says you have to split all your earnings with him, fifty-fifty. That's highway robbery! You also owe him for the jobs he gets you, even if you don't show up."

"He never told me that," Theresa said in a wavering voice.

"Well, that's what you've gotten into," her father said. "He says either you go through with it or he wants five hundred dollars to tear up the contract."

To be in Theresa's position can be scary. Whether the creditor—that is, the one to whom you owe money or services—is an individual, a small business, or a large corporation, they will try hard to get what they bargained for. They may send you letters demanding payment, make repeated calls to you on the telephone, or threaten to take you to court.

In the face of such pressure, many young people and their families find it easier to pay the penalty than to fight the system. They do what is demanded of them and sometimes learn an expensive lesson from the experience. But the easy way out isn't always the best way. By giving in to the pressure of a creditor, you may be cheating yourself of a legal right to avoid the duty created by the contract.

The morning after speaking to Mark, Theresa's father stopped in at their neighborhood legal assistance office. One of the lawyers there invited him to sit down, took his name, address, and a few other statistics and heard his story. It took only a short discussion of Theresa's right of voidability to put her father's mind at ease.

Perhaps the most important thing you can learn about contracts is that they work both ways. In every legal rule there is a requirement of good faith by both sides. This means simply that even if differences arise, the parties are supposed to treat each other fairly and honestly. If they don't, they are breaking the spirit of the law and no judge or lawyer in the land would approve of their activity.

Because of this principle of good faith, you cannot just make and then tear up contracts when it suits you. You have a duty to yourself and those you deal with to think before you sign on the dotted line or hand over your money.

As Mary Beth found out when she used her sister's I.D., voidability is a privilege that can be lost by improper conduct. If misused by those it was designed to protect, it may someday disappear altogether.

4

Putting a Roof Over Your Head— And Keeping It There

From the subject of contract rights to that of leases and other housing rental agreements is a short and logical step. A lease, which is defined by legal dictionaries as "any agreement which gives rise to the relationship of landlord and tenant," is really nothing more than a specialized type of contract. It can entitle you to use or occupy any amount of land or water, a building, house, store, or just a single room. It can run for a week, a month, or a number of years if both parties want it to. In addition to the basic right to occupy the leased property for the time agreed upon, the lease can put special duties on either the landlord or the tenant, such as the responsibility to paint the apartment or make repairs.

50

These are the obvious parts of a lease, written for all to see. If, for example, it says on page one "Ms. Beverly Harrison hereby agrees to rent the house at 100 Ocean Drive, Long Beach, California, for the period of one year at a monthly rate of $500," there can be no doubt what she has contracted for and how much she is to pay.

But there is much more to this unique sort of contract than the words that appear on its pages. Contained in every lease is a wide variety of unwritten conditions that are implied from other sources. The most important of these are housing codes and regulations which are made part of the law by local legislatures, and the nationwide "common law" rules of landlord-tenant relations that come from the decisions of American and English courts over the past several hundred years.

But, you may ask, is there anything special about a lease that applies to minors only? The answer, other than the voidability right that we discussed in the last chapter, is no. Still, two important considerations make a discussion of tenants' rights appropriate in this book.

The first might best be summed up in the old saying, "forewarned is forearmed." Sooner or later, most people will find themselves in a real estate office signing a lease for an apartment or house. Early in life, very few people have the money necessary to buy their own home. Therefore, the best time to learn what you're entitled to under a rental agreement is *before* you legally commit yourself.

The second reason is that today, more than ever before, people under eighteen are leaving their parents' home and trying to make it on their own. When they do, putting a roof over their heads is foremost among a host of new problems. If you happen to be one of these young people, knowing the basics of leasing is more than just theory—it is an essential fact of life.

Isabelle, for instance, might have found knowledge of these facts helpful when she moved into her first apartment. She was three months away from her seventeenth birthday when she went away to college in Ithaca, New York. Dormitory living was not required, so she got together with Susan, another freshman, and rented the ground floor of a house near the campus. Their landlord was a retired old man who was so hard of hearing that the girls had to shout when they spoke to him. He lived on the second floor. The house was on a tree-lined, dead-end street and seemed a perfect place to concentrate on schoolwork.

The perfection lasted only until the third night. About eleven o'clock in the evening, hammering started. Half an hour later it was followed by the sound of a buzz saw that rattled all the bottles on the bedroom dresser. Then the hammering was back, broken only by an occasional *crash* as something heavy dropped to the floor.

By two-thirty in the morning Isabelle could stand the noise no longer and went upstairs to complain. Her speech about an early class the next morning fell, quite literally, on deaf ears. The old man simply could not tell what a ruckus he was creating. He nodded sympathetically at everything she said, but five minutes later was back at his woodworking. The din went on for another hour.

By the end of the first month the midnight symphony had been repeated at least a dozen times. Even on quiet nights the girls lost sleep wondering if the disturbance would begin again. Protesting did no good. Isabelle's temper became shorter with each week and dark rings began to show under Susan's eyes.

Finally, at their wits' end, the girls told the old man they were moving out. But he only shook his head with a scowl. "There's nothing in that lease," he told them, "that says I can't do what I want in my place whenever I want to. And if it ain't written down, it's my business and nobody else's."

"Let me tell you something," he went on, leaning forward and wagging a finger. "If you two run out on this lease I can find you easily enough through the college. I'll take you to court and the judge will make you pay for the whole year!"

The landlord was wrong. The fact that the lease says nothing about noise doesn't mean he can create as much disturbance as he likes. One of the most important unwritten conditions in every lease is called a "covenant of quiet enjoyment." The word "covenant" means any agreement between the parties. You, as tenant, have a right to use the rented premises for any normal activity—such as eating, sleeping, or studying—without interference from the landlord.

Making too much noise isn't the only way a landlord can break the covenant of quiet enjoyment. The result is the same if a defective old furnace fills your apartment with smoke or if the landlord piles the garbage under your window and the smell is unbearable. Hundreds of things can interfere with your use and enjoyment of the place you've rented.

What can you do about it? The answer is simple: you can move out, just as Susan and Isabelle planned to do. Once you are out of the house for good, your obligation to pay rent stops. Since it was the landlord's fault you had to leave, it would be grossly unfair to allow him to collect more money from you. No court would allow this to happen.

There are many other mishaps that can make a rented

53

house or apartment useless but can't as easily be blamed on the landlord. One good example happened in New Jersey not long ago. A businessman leased the ground floor of an office building for use as a training center. For several weeks after he moved in, everything went smoothly. Then one day during a rainstorm he discovered that water was seeping into the offices through invisible cracks in the walls and foundation. The problem worsened with each downpour. The last straw came on the morning of a big sales meeting, when he arrived to find the place awash under five inches of water.

"What is it we're supposed to be selling," joked one of the trainees when he saw the mess, "water wings?"

When the businessman removed his equipment and stopped paying rent, the landlord took him to court. "How can I be responsible?" the landlord argued. "The tenant had every opportunity to see the condition of the building. He should have known what he was getting into. If he rented a leaky office, it's his own fault."

But the court disagreed. "It has come to be recognized," the judge wrote, "that ordinarily the tenant does not have as much knowledge of the condition of the premises as the landlord. A prospective tenant cannot be expected to know if the plumbing or wiring systems are adequate. Nor should he be expected to hire experts to advise him."

This means that you have a right to rely on the landlord's word that a house or apartment has no hidden defects. Even more important, the landlord has a duty to tell you before you sign the lease whether the place has any "invisible" problems. You are not expected to take your chances on whether you'll get what you are paying for.

If the landlord knows of a problem, he must inform you of it.

Local housing codes are another important but unwritten part of your lease. Every city in the country has a housing inspection department which enforces certain minimum standards of utility service. For example, your home must receive sufficient heat during the winter. If the temperature falls below legal limits, you can call the bureau for assistance. They can also help when the landlord doesn't provide running water, adequate sewage disposal, or electricity.

But do your rights end at the apartment door? The answer to this question almost cost Nicholas his life. He lived in a third story walk-up apartment. It was not a new building and the stairways were narrow and steep. It was necessary to grasp the banister for security. Each flight of stairs was illuminated at night by a single bare bulb in the ceiling, but this left the hallways dim at best.

One evening Nick came in to find the ground-floor light burned out. The fixture was too high for him to reach, so the next morning he called the landlord about replacing it. The secretary replied that "the super" would "take care of it." Two days later, however, the stairs were still in darkness.

That night Nick arrived home about eight-thirty, after dinner at a friend's house. He made a mental note to call the landlord again as he groped for the railing. When he reached the third step he thought he heard a noise behind him and turned slightly.

It was already too late. Something hard glanced off the side of his head and smashed into his left shoulder. As he fell forward another terrific blow landed in his stomach.

For an instant he seemed weightless, spinning. Then his head struck the edge of a stair and everything went quiet and black.

Later that night he awoke in a hospital emergency room. His wallet was gone, and he had several large bruises and a dislocated shoulder. But the thought foremost in his mind was to find out who was responsible for the broken light that had made the mugging possible.

The stairway of your apartment building is legally termed a "common area." It doesn't belong to any one apartment and no single tenant is paying rent for it. Therefore the residents are not responsible for its upkeep. It is the landlord's duty to keep it safe for you and your guests to use: lighted at night, and free of holes, broken boards, or shaky banisters that might cause injury. The same goes for halls, elevators, and rest rooms of office buildings or other places of business.

Tenants are not without their own responsibilities under a rental housing agreement. Your most basic obligation is to pay rent when it is due. Not doing so is a serious breach of the contract you signed with the landlord. As owner of the property, he can demand his money and have you evicted if you don't pay.

Most leases also provide for a security deposit. This is a sum you're required to leave with the landlord when you move in. It usually equals one or two months' rent. If all goes well during the lease term, you get the money back. But if you're evicted, or you "split" without paying rent, the landlord is entitled to keep as much of the deposit as it takes to cover his losses.

Another important duty is to read your lease before you

sign it. Because it is essentially a contract, the words of a rental agreement control what both sides have to do. Any of the rules we've discussed in this chapter can be altered by the text of a lease. Nicholas' lease, for example, could have contained a line saying, "Tenants are responsible for maintenance and any condition of common areas." If this were the case, Nick would have been responsible for fixing the light bulb. A special clause in Susan and Isabelle's lease could have allowed their landlord to hammer all night if he wanted. Therefore, common caution dictates that you go over a rental agreement line by line before signing.

Finally, no matter how careful you are along the way there are often disagreements between landlords and tenants. Plumbing fixtures or major appliances may remain broken for weeks. Snow-covered steps may not be shoveled. An unreliable elevator may cause you inconvenience. Legally, it might be up to the landlord to correct all of these problems. But sometimes even *finding* your landlord after you've moved in is an impossible task. Over the years, so many landlords have ignored their tenants' gripes that their profession has come to rank only slightly above a dogcatcher's in social respectability.

Because of this, your building or neighborhood may have a tenants' association that will help you to get action on a complaint. In addition, your city's housing inspection department can lend a hand when your landlord won't give satisfaction.

Seeking aid from organizations like these is never wrong. They are there to assist in enforcing your rights to a safe, clean, decent place in which to live or work. But you must take the first step. Unless you call them in, none of these agencies can help you or accomplish their job of policing local housing conditions. As with all the other legal conditions we will discuss, it boils down to this: if *you* don't stand up for your rights, no one else will.

5
Your Responsibilities to Others

Ginger lives in Seattle with her widowed father, whose business takes him out of town several days a week. While he's gone Ginger likes to invite her friends over for parties. There isn't any room for parking on her narrow street, so when the kids arrive she tells them to put their cars on the grass in front of nearby houses. But her neighbors are furious when they find their lawns crisscrossed with tire tracks.

Vince also lives in a neighborhood of single-family homes. The house next door is owned by Charley, an older man who is always puttering around the yard planting bushes or setting up decorations. One day Charley installed a powerful floodlight over his driveway. "He told me it was to ward off burglars," Vince says. "But the darn thing was shining right in my bedroom window and kept me awake all night. I complained time and again but the old guy wouldn't listen. So one night I just took a rock and put it out myself."

When the U.S. Constitution was written two centuries ago, most Americans lived on farms. Your neighbor's house was usually far out of sight and there was little likelihood of disturbing him. Today, like Ginger and Vince, most of us live in houses only a few feet apart or in apartment buildings where other people are literally on top of us. Living in this kind of environment means that we must look out for the rights of others as much as ourselves.

Every "right" that we speak of in this book carries with it a duty not to infringe on another person's rights. Our freedom of speech isn't a freedom to shout someone else down. The right to decide issues for yourself doesn't mean you can force others to adopt your way of thinking. The liberty to travel doesn't include trampling on our neighbors' property.

Everyone knows that if you go onto another person's land without their permission, you're trespassing. English law books from as far back as the fifteenth century speak of "the King's writ of trespass," making it one of the oldest surviving legal complaints. In our examples, however, neither Ginger nor Vince actually walked on their neighbors' property. Ginger simply instructed others to put their cars on the grass. Vince threw a stone which landed on Charley's grounds, but didn't go there himself. Is this still trespass?

Yes. You can be taken to court for trespass without actually stepping onto another's land. In directing other people to park in the wrong place, Ginger is just as guilty as if she'd done it herself. What Vince did with the rock is the same as going onto the property himself to break the light. If he had sprayed water from a garden hose onto Charley's land the result would be the same.

An intrusion onto your neighbor's property need not be intentional to be a trespass. Suppose Vince is building something on his own land. During the construction, a wooden board accidentally falls over the boundary into Charley's yard and smashes his light. Despite the fact that Vince didn't mean to cross the line, he is still technically a trespasser and must replace the lamp.

On the other hand, if Vince were walking by Charley's house on the public sidewalk and should be pushed onto Charley's land by another person, he wouldn't be trespassing. The reason is that he would have been powerless to control his action while someone else took over. The third person would now be the trespasser.

Certain types of people do have the privilege of going onto your property without your permission. For example, a policeman cannot be kept off private land if he is making a proper arrest. Firemen may go almost anywhere in the performance of their duty. It is assumed, unless you specifically state otherwise, that mail carriers, oil delivery men, and other service people can enter your yard to do their job. In an emergency even a private citizen can go across your land to protect his or her own life or safety.

Right after his high school graduation, Fred moved out of his parents' house and took a small apartment in the city. "The best thing about being on my own," he says, "is that I can do whatever I want in my place. If I feel like listening to records all night, I just put 'em on and crank it up loud." There's only one problem: Fred's moonlight music sessions are driving his neighbors nuts.

The law views loud noises, lights like Charley's, smells, smoke, vibrations, or dust differently from the physical intrusions we call trespass. They are known by the same word you would probably use—"nuisances." A nuisance need not be restricted to those living close by. If Fred's stereo were powerful enough to send guitar chords booming for blocks in every direction, anyone who lost sleep would have a right to complain.

However, the chances of being taken to court for a nuisance are less than for trespass. The reason is that trespass is much easier to prove: you either went onto your neighbor's property or you didn't. The legal standard for nuisance is much more complex. Not only must it be shown that Fred is playing his stereo at night, but also that he is doing it at an unreasonable hour, at too high a volume, that the neighbors are losing sleep because of it, and that anyone else in the neighbors' position would likewise lose sleep.

Why all these conditions? To protect your rights against oversensitive neighbors. If it were easy to prove a nuisance, someone who was an exceptionally light sleeper might take you to court for sneezing at night. Another person might sue you because he didn't like the color of your house. Without legal safeguards we could become slaves to our neighbors' tastes and feelings.

Like trespass, nuisances can be caused indirectly. Let's say the fellow across the street erects a thirty-foot statue of Buddha in his yard. Looking at it may not please you, but that doesn't make it a nuisance. However, if hundreds of religious pilgrims begin to visit the shrine daily and your quiet street becomes choked with cars and people, you may have a legitimate reason to go to court.

Bucky and Matt are walking home from school when they see Dennis coming in the opposite direction. "This guy is a real wimp," Matt says to his friend. "Watch this." He takes a knife out of his back pocket and holds it in the air.

"Hey turkey," he yells at Dennis. "C'mere. I'm gonna cut you."

The other boy, obviously scared, stops in his tracks and stares at Matt. "What do you want?" he says.

"Just a little cut," Matt says, approaching him. "Just wanna carve my initials in your arm, that's all."

Dennis turns and starts to run. After only a few steps he stumbles and falls, banging his head on the sidewalk. Matt and Bucky walk away, laughing. But a friend of Dennis' who saw the incident helps him up and takes him to a hospital where X-rays reveal a concussion.

This is a classic case of assault. While TV police shows have made the expression "assault and battery" familiar, most people still don't know that it stands for two distinct offenses which are not always found together. Knowing the difference between assault and battery might keep what you think is a harmless prank from turning into a legal mess.

The legal definition of an assault is any intentional act which is seen by the victim and causes him to think he will be hurt. His reaction need not be what the acting person intended to happen. In our example, Matt gave Dennis ample reason to be afraid by showing the knife and making a threat. He intended to scare Dennis. The fact that he never really planned to use the knife and never touched Dennis doesn't make this any less of an assault.

The element of physical contact changes an assault into a battery. If Matt had grabbed Dennis or touched him with the knife he would have committed a battery as well as an assault. Of course, you don't inflict a battery every time you shake someone's hand. To qualify, the touching must be without the other person's permission or against their will.

But suppose Matt had just been showing his knife to Bucky when he held it out and hadn't even seen Dennis coming. If Dennis had reacted the same way at the sight of the weapon and hurt himself, would Matt still be guilty of assault? No. The missing requirement is that Matt must have intended to put Dennis in fear of being touched. If he didn't know Dennis was there it is impossible that he could have meant to scare him.

It isn't necessary to show superior force in committing assault or battery. In fact, a pro football player could take a dwarf to court on these grounds despite the fact that the little guy clearly couldn't do him any harm. The root of these offenses is the unauthorized touching itself and not whether the touch will hurt.

The legal consequences of assault or battery can be severe. You may be ordered by the court to pay for your victim's medical treatment. In addition, you could be charged for his inconvenience and emotional upset resulting from the incident. Lawyers call this "pain and suffering." This item alone can amount to thousands of dollars.

Many teen-agers—not all of them bullies like Matt— find it amusing to throw a scare into other people. Usually the game is harmless. But when someone unexpectedly gets hurt, it can be very rough on the person responsible. Insisting that "we were only kidding around" is no help if your victim wasn't in on the joke. If you don't think twice about the possible danger in your pranks, the joke could end up being on *you*.

And you won't find it very funny.

6

"Get a Job"

For some the hunt begins as early as November. Others wait until after New Year's. But by March tens of thousands of teen-agers are pounding the streets of their towns or mailing applications to vacation spots from Big Sur to Cape Cod in search of a summer job.

Every year the quest becomes more difficult. Government statistics show that unemployment in the sixteen-to-nineteen age bracket routinely runs over seventeen percent. Among minorities the rate is even higher. The stiffest competition is in the aging and financially troubled cities, such as Baltimore, Cincinnati, Los Angeles, and New York, where over one fifth of the young people are unable to find jobs.

Although we are fond of saying that every American has a right to work, in practice this "right" is no stronger than the market for your services. No business will hire you unless it needs more people to handle its trade. When the trade slows down and less money comes in, employers begin looking for ways to cut expenses. Reducing the payroll is often easiest. Among the first to go are "unskilled" positions such as waitresses, salesmen, gasoline pumpers, delivery boys, and clerks—posts usually available to teen-agers.

Even where jobs exist, the odds of landing one are getting tougher. Kids used to competing with other students or part-timers are now finding themselves up against older people who are out of work, unions in trades like auto workers and longshoremen that close their ranks to summer help, or other young people who have taken a year or two off before college to work full-time.

Government decisions also keep you out of certain areas. The horrible child labor conditions of the 1800s spawned many laws regulating the kind of work you can do and limiting the hours in a working day. New legislation and amendments to old laws keep the rules up to date.

The federal Fair Labor Standards Act, in force in all fifty states, lists over a dozen types of employment that are considered too dangerous for people under eighteen. They include almost any kind of night work, motor vehicle driving, logging and sawmill jobs, wrecking and demolition, mining and excavation activities, and certain hazardous agricultural activities.

In addition, every state now has its own child labor laws. Illinois makes it illegal for anyone under sixteen to work between 7 P.M. and 7 A.M., more than eight hours in one day, or more than forty-eight hours per week. If you're under eighteen, New York prohibits you from being a window cleaner, locomotive driver, meat-packer, slaughter-house employee, or a worker in several other risky occupations. Many other states outlaw employment during school hours if you're under sixteen. Most states have no restrictions on working around your own home and make special provisions for jobs usually performed by young children, like delivering newspapers or picking vegetables.

But even if you've found an opening in a field you're permitted to enter, there are often more legal hurdles to clear. As my young friend Ruth discovered, most states have a series of steps you must go through before you can start work.

Ruth was sixteen the summer she got a job as a sales-person in Gold's department store. Her older sister had worked there a few years before, so she had a pretty good idea of the building's layout and the correct sales procedure. She also remembered her sister's getting some sort of legal authorization before beginning the job, but couldn't recall exactly what was required. She asked the store's personnel department what to do.

They directed her to the local post office. There Ruth applied for a social security card. Every worker in the nation is required to have one of these cards. Each card carries a number that stays with you for the rest of your life. Under the U.S. Social Security program, money is taken out of your paycheck every week and sent to Washington. When you reach retirement age, this money plus your employer's contribution is returned to you monthly to provide a continuing income. Your number will also be used to identify you in colleges, banks, and other institutions.

Ruth's next stop was a state office building, where she

got a youth employment permit. Many states require these special papers for workers under eighteen because they assist in keeping track of young people employed in the state and in enforcement of child labor laws. Application forms can often be picked up in public schools.

While it isn't difficult to get an employment certificate, there are usually some firm requirements: you must provide legal proof of your age (a birth certificate or baptismal record), have written permission from your parent or guardian, and go through a medical examination to demonstrate good health. Frequently the state will also provide you with a form to be filled out by your employer, stating that you will be hired and describing the sort of job you will be required to do.

Armed with these documents, Ruth began work at Gold's in late June. Having complied with the formalities of the law, she was now eligible for its protections. One of these protections let her know how much she would be paid even though the figure was never actually named when she was hired. This is widely known as the minimum wage and it applies equally to teen-agers and adults.

What you may not know is that there are actually several different minimum wage rates. The broadest one is the federal minimum hourly wage, effective in all fifty states. As of January 1, 1979, it stood at $2.90 and was scheduled to rise by 20¢ in the first month of 1980 and 25¢ to $3.35 in 1981.

Each state also has the power to set its own minimum wage level. Many states have coordinated their law with the federal government to avoid conflict. Others have followed an independent course. If a state requires higher minimum wages than those set by the U.S. Congress, all businesses in the state must pay the higher rate. If a state's wage standard is lower, small businesses—those taking in less than $250,000 per year—can follow the local scale but larger enterprises must pay the national minimum.

There is yet another minimum wage created by special law in some states. It permits some small businesses to pay slightly less than the normal minimum to students and employees under eighteen. A telephone call to the information bureau or minimum wage office of your state's Labor Department will let you know which pay rate applies in your situation.

Not all jobs are covered by these regulations. Traditionally some farm tasks, yard work, golf-course caddying, housecleaning, and other irregular occupations are exempt from minimum wage requirements. However, it isn't uncommon to find employers who *are* subject to the law paying some young workers less than the set amount. Stranger still, the kids aren't complaining about it. Why don't they stand up for their rights?

The reason involves supply and demand, as we discussed earlier. The game is called "paying under the table." It's illegal and no responsible attorney would endorse it, but some employers and young workers play it willingly. Let's say that the owner of a flower shop is interested in increasing his business. He figures that hiring a delivery boy will enable him to sell an extra $40 worth of flowers every day. But the plants will cost him $15 from his suppliers and paying the delivery boy the minimum wage of $2.90 for eight hours a day will add $23.20. This makes the florist's total expenses $38.20, leaving him only $1.80 profit on $40.00 worth of trade (4.5%). At that rate it is hardly worth his trouble.

The teen-ager looking for work is interested in making as much money as possible in the short time he has available—usually weekends or school vacations. He is painfully aware that getting the minimum wage doesn't mean he'll be taking home $2.90 an hour. After federal taxes, state taxes, and social security payments are taken out of his paycheck he will wind up quite a bit short. But since the alternative is unemployment, he'll take whatever job he can get.

Payment under the table can make money for both parties. The florist pays his delivery boy $2.60, saving himself 30¢ per hour. This brings the daily profit up to $4.20, a considerable improvement over the $1.80 he figured on. The worker also receives a little more than he would get by obeying the law, since no taxes are deducted from his pay.

The key to this is that everything is done in cash. There are no records and the delivery boy isn't on the official payroll. As a result, the florist and his employee can be almost certain that no government agency would waste its time bringing them to court for the few tax dollars lost through this deception.

While this kind of arrangement, though illegal, is widely practiced by small enterprises, it is out of bounds for big businesses. The extra income generated by paying cash to one or two workers would seem pitifully small to a major manufacturer or retail store and cheating on a larger scale might result in a costly government lawsuit.

When Ruth began work at Gold's she was put on the normal payroll at the minimum wage. All went smoothly until one Friday when she happened to be with Tony, a boy hired with Ruth to do the same job, when they picked up their paychecks. "The only bad thing about paydays," Tony was saying as they ripped open their envelopes, "is that I know where practically every penny is going even before I get the money. Twenty-five dollars a week has to be for car payments, fifty gets put toward college tuition, and that only leaves thirty-five as spending cash."

"Thirty-five?" Ruth said. "How much overtime do you have to put in to get that?"

"None at all. That's my pay."

Ruth stopped. "Wait a minute, that totals a hundred and ten dollars a week. I only get one hundred and six, and if we're both making minimum wage—"

"But we're not," Tony interrupted. "All the guys who work with me get ten cents an hour more than that, same as I do. I thought everybody got the same amount."

So did Ruth. But after questioning most of the summer employees she discovered that all the men were receiving a higher wage than women doing the same tasks. She felt cheated and outraged, and decided to find out whether Gold's different pay scales were legal. Several phone calls led her to the local district office of the U.S. Equal Employment Opportunity Commission, which handles reports of job discrimination all over the country.

The law recognizes many valid reasons for paying different sums to people doing the same job. For example, some employees may be more experienced or may have worked for a longer period and received annual raises. But the law also states that some traits may not be used to justify different treatment under any circumstances: these are race, religion, nationality, and sex. Under this rule, paying a woman differently for doing the same thing as a man is the same as making black people sit at different tables in restaurants or forcing Jews to wear yellow stars on their clothing. Sex discrimination on the job is illegal and the federal government is supposed to investigate reports of it. Men and women of all ages have a right to equal pay for equal work.

Ruth learned that she and all the other women in Gold's summer staff were entitled to the ten cents per hour they'd missed since starting work. The next day she went to discuss the matter with the store's personnel director.

"You don't understand the system," the older man said. "We have a lot of boys doing heavy work like unloading trucks. We pay them more for that."

"They aren't the ones I'm talking about," Ruth insisted. "I mean boys who are out front selling just like me."

"If we paid the salesmen less than the boys in the stockroom," the director said in a weary tone, "nobody would want to do it. We have to attract people."

Ruth sensed that she was getting a runaround. She tried not to sound emotional or scared. "Well, when I call the EEOC lawyer I'll tell him that. I *did* promise to let him know what you said."

The director stared at her woodenly, without speaking. Ruth tried to guess what he was thinking. She knew that complaining to an official agency about possibly illegal working conditions was proper. She had been within her rights in going to the Commission for help. If they fired her for this reason she could sue Gold's and recover all her lost wages. But Ruth worried that her boss might invent some other excuse to let her go. What could she do if they branded her "incompetent" or a "troublemaker"?

Finally the director spoke. "Hold off on that call," he

said. "Let me get back to you on this." He still wore a poker face and Ruth left his office wondering if she had just talked herself out of a job.

Two weeks later the women employed for the summer found something extra in their pay envelopes: a ten-cent raise and another check making up the difference since the day they'd been hired.

What if Ruth were to be laid off for some valid reason? When an adult loses his job and has trouble finding a new one, government unemployment insurance provides money for essentials such as food, rent, and clothing. Under the law in most states, minors may also collect unemployment (though a few places set fourteen as the minimum age). All you have to do to qualify for payments is meet the same standards as an adult.

At first glance this seems fair. But it is one area where equality actually works against you. The catch is that government standards usually include a minimum length of full-time employment or minimum earnings in the year preceding your claim for unemployment compensation. In Massachusetts, for example, you must have earned at least $1200 and thirty times your weekly benefit rate to be eligible. Other states have fifteen- or twenty-week employment requirements.

These rules make it almost impossible for a young person who hasn't worked for very long or who attends school to collect unemployment compensation. Workers in certain types of businesses are also not covered. Depending on the state, church employees, some farm workers, domestic help, children who work in a family-owned business, and employees of nonprofit organizations may not qualify. Even the circumstances of your leaving the job have an effect:

if you are fired for misconduct or quit voluntarily you may also be excluded from unemployment payments.

This chapter has been largely concerned with money. That's because money is the reason most people go to work in the first place. In the past, however, it was common for children to work for years without seeing a single penny of what they earned. The salary was paid directly to their parents because youngsters were regarded as their possessions. Today minors are recognized as independent in many ways, with rights of their own. Does this mean that parents no longer have any right to touch the money you earn?

The answer is no. In many cases a mother or father may claim the child's wages. This rule has practical application among many families that need the extra income of children to make ends meet. But the law doesn't restrict this power to low-income households. As in colonial times, selfish parents can legally force a dependent minor to turn over what he or she earns—no matter how well-off they are. The rule is a holdover from the days when all children were little more than servants whose wages would compensate their parents for the cost of raising them. Though parents can no longer sell children by placing an ad in the newspaper, it is still true that a dependent minor may be forced to turn over what he earns to his parents.

How can you retain control over your money? You may be helped by the state you live in. California, New York, and some other states require employers to pay wages directly to their young workers unless notified to the contrary by parents or guardians.

Otherwise, it's up to you. Obviously the most practical method is to agree with your parents that what you earn will be yours to keep. This agreement can be oral. If it is written, so much the better. But third and most importantly, it can be inferred from actions taken in the past. If you have earned money before and been allowed to keep it all, this fact may be used to show that it was "understood" the pay would be yours.

If you get married under age eighteen and move out of your parents' house, it is likely that what you earn will be beyond their reach. The same applies if you enlist in the armed forces.

A common way of safeguarding money is by opening a bank account. Once you deposit a paycheck, cash or other funds in a savings account in your own name no one can touch it but you. If the bank allowed anyone else to do so it would land in terrible legal trouble. However, some banks are reluctant to deal with anyone under eighteen because of the unique contract provisions that apply to them (the document you sign to open the account is a contract). They will insist that minors open a "trust" or "joint account" with an older person. The bad part of this arrangement is that it allows someone else access to all the money held in the account.

Many banks, especially in large towns and cities, will open an individual account for anyone who can produce a social security number, sign his name, and show an acceptable form of identification. Some banks don't even require a social security number to start a savings account. A birth certificate, school I.D., or even a library card will usually do. Afterward you may deposit and withdraw money from the account whenever you choose without fear that your parents or anyone else will get to it.

7
Drugs and Driving

It seemed as though everyone in town was throwing a party on the night after Staples High School's homecoming football game. Bruce and Heidi, both fifteen, wanted to visit as many as they could. At Joyce's house they ran across their friend Peter, who was sixteen, and persuaded him to drive them to another celebration.

A lot of the kids at Joyce's party had been smoking marijuana. To keep up the good mood, Bruce brought a "road joint" with him. The three passed it around as they drove.

Just after pulling away from an intersection, however, the car was suddenly bathed in blue light. Almost at once there were policemen on either side. The kids were ordered out, frisked and bundled into the back seat of a police cruiser.

Their car was searched. The half-smoked joint was removed from an ashtray and kept as evidence.

The three kids were too shocked and scared to do anything but stare through the wire mesh of their cage. Within five minutes they were on the way to police headquarters.

"There's only one thing worse than being busted," I was told by a young Bostonian who has been to juvenile court several times, "and that is being busted when you're high. There's no way you can deal with it."

His words brought nods of agreement from the group of young people around us. Yet it is far from unusual for minors to find themselves in police hands with their thinking clouded by dope smoking. Why?

Part of the reason is marijuana's ready availability. You can buy an ounce of it—or more—in every school, neighborhood, and community in the nation. It isn't expensive. In addition, young people no longer believe that pot smoking will lead straight to addiction, insanity, violence, or sterility.

As a result, marijuana use continues to grow among teenagers. A 1978 report in *New York* magazine stated that over fifty percent of the seventh- to twelfth-graders in that state have tried the drug. Statistics from other states are similar.

Another part of the answer is that penalties for use or possession of grass have become less severe in recent years. As of mid-1978, eleven states had ceased handing out criminal sentences for minor marijuana offenses: Alaska, Maine, Colorado, California, Ohio, Minnesota, Mississippi, Nebraska, New York, North Carolina, and Oregon. In many other states, people caught for the first time are usually let off with a light fine or simply told to participate in a local "rehabilitation" or "drug education" program.

Bruce, Peter, and Heidi are only a few of the thousands of kids arrested annually for smoking pot. But this fact is of little comfort to them. They are only thinking of one thing: What happens now?

Almost every state would send the three teen-agers to juvenile court. As discussed in Chapter Two, this court was created solely to handle cases involving young people. Its rules and procedures differ in many respects from those of an adult criminal court. One of the most important differences is that the normal penalties for offenses such as robbery, vandalism, and marijuana possession do not apply in juvenile proceedings.

If, at the conclusion of their hearing, the judge feels that Bruce, Peter, and Heidi violated the law by smoking marijuana, he will pronounce them "delinquent." After that, he alone will decide the "disposition" of the case—that is, what punishment to order. A juvenile court judge isn't restricted to the usual adult remedies of imprisonment or paying a fine. He can order that a minor be put on probation, be committed to a state institution such as a reform school, training school, or even an adult jail, or be placed in a foster home.

Is it possible for a young person to predict how severe his or her punishment will be by looking at the penalties prescribed for marijuana use by adults? Generally, no. While the liberality of your state's law may influence the judge's attitude, criminal penalties do not provide strict guidelines for treatment of juvenile offenders.

For example, it is quite possible for a youngster who lives in Kentucky—a state whose penalties for marijuana possession are relatively light—to receive a harsher judgment than a minor in Arizona, where adults can get ten years in state prison and a $50,000 fine if caught with a joint.

Does this mean that a juvenile court judge can hand out any punishment he likes? Not exactly. The legislature in each state has written laws which limit the judge to a specific list of dispositions. From this list the judge may choose the penalty he or she thinks most appropriate.

If you're arrested on a marijuana charge, the juvenile court may simply send you home with a warning. *But don't count on it.* The national trend toward decriminalization of pot is no guarantee that you won't be sent to reform school.

Bruce, Peter and Heidi will not have to worry about the disposition of their case if the judge does not find them delinquent. In making his decision, the judge will consider two main factors: testimony from both sides and the joint taken from Peter's car.

Producing the marijuana in court scores a very important point against the young people. It is physical proof that what the policemen saw and smelled during the arrest was actually an illegal drug. Yet this vital evidence was not taken from any of the accused kids. It was found during a search of their automobile.

Are such searches legal?

It is common knowledge that, under most circumstances, a cop needs a search warrant to enter and examine your home. To obtain such a warrant, the police must go before a court official and get approval before the search takes place. The warrant must describe in specific terms the place to be searched and list what the police are looking for.

The Supreme Court has made several exceptions to this general rule, however. One of these exceptions concerns searches made during a valid arrest. In a 1969 case, the Court decided that the police have a right to search a limited area around their suspect without a search warrant. "There is ample justification," wrote the Supreme Court, "for a search of the arrestee's person and the area 'within his immediate control'—construing that phrase to mean the area from within which he might gain possession of a weapon or destructible evidence."

Although that particular case did not involve an automobile, its words seem tailor-made for highway arrests. A car is literally within the driver's control whenever it is being operated, and is full of places where weapons or evidence may be hidden from view yet easily reached. In addition, it can be quickly removed (along with anything it contains) if police lack the power to search it right away.

Therefore if you are arrested while driving, your car can be legally searched. This can happen either before or after you are taken to the police station.

May this search include the trunk or glove compartment of the vehicle? Yes. Because these places are so often used to hide illegal items, many courts have approved examination of their contents during an arrest.

If police consider the automobile itself to be evidence, they can impound it and conduct a search later. Good examples of this include the seizure of suspected hit-and-run or getaway cars.

Can the police stop you on any pretext and then, if they find marijuana in the car, "bust" you? Yes, but any evidence taken from a car detained without "probable cause" that illegal activity was going on cannot be used in court.

Technically, automobiles are private property. But the law does not treat them with the same respect it accords houses. Why? In 1974 the Supreme Court said, "One has a lesser expectation of privacy in a motor vehicle because its function is transportation and it seldom serves as one's residence. . . . It travels public thoroughfares where both its occupants and its contents are in plain view."

In other words, your car isn't your castle. Police know this, so automobile searches are part of their regular procedure. Judges know it too, so they will accept evidence like the joint from Peter's car more easily than evidence from a warrantless house search.

And, for your own protection, you should remember it.

8
Young People and Sex-The Unanswered Questions

A decade ago there would have been very little to say in a chapter on your sexual rights.

In the late 1960s magazines, radio, and TV were loudly announcing that a "sexual revolution" and a "new morality" were sweeping the country. Young people, they said, were leading the way.

Whether this was right or wrong, there is no question that popular attitudes toward sex became more liberal. But the laws had not yet begun to reflect the social changes. Kids who were sexually active took risks that are both unwise and unnecessary today.

If you had been a teen-ager in those years, birth control would have been difficult. Until 1965, Connecticut and some other states made it a crime for anyone to use contraceptives. It was only in 1972 that the U.S. Supreme Court decided it was illegal to deny all unmarried people the right to make use of birth control devices.

At that time neither a minor nor anyone else had the legal right to end a pregnancy. Until 1973 there were only two ways for a woman "in trouble" to get an abortion: go to a licensed doctor who was willing to risk imprisonment if he got caught performing the illegal operation, or pay an exorbitant fee to a quack and hope he knew what he was doing. Using these methods, many rich women had illegal abortions and many poor ones died.

In recent years things have changed dramatically. The subject of sex, which used to be considered unfit for discussion, is now being talked about in schools and argued about in courts. The result of all this, so far, has been to expand your legal rights in most areas of sex-related activity.

THE AGE OF CONSENT

This basic aspect of the law has changed very little in recent years. All fifty states and the District of Columbia have laws which fix a minimum age when a woman may agree to have sexual relations with a man. This is known as the "age of consent." If you are a girl living in Pennsylvania, for example, you cannot legally have sex until age sixteen. The same age applies in Colorado, Indiana, Massachusetts, and many other states. In New York both a man and a woman must be at least seventeen. In North Carolina and Mississippi, a girl can consent as early as age twelve.

But law and real life do not always run side by side. While these regulations are just as valid as those which prohibit speeding or stealing, they don't seem to stop many young people under legal age from engaging in sex.

Do you know your state's age of consent? If not, you aren't alone. Few kids know the legal age and even fewer worry about getting caught. In the words of one Massachusetts boy whose girl friend is fifteen, "What's gonna happen? Are the police gonna surround my house and bust into the bedroom?"

Of course, that idea is silly. But so is the notion that age of consent laws are never enforced. Sexual activity below the legal age can result in very serious trouble. In almost all states any boy can be taken to court and charged with the crime of *statutory rape*. Though "rape" may seem the wrong word to describe something to which you both agreed, that is what the minimum age laws mean. A girl below the age of consent cannot really agree to having sex, no matter what she says before or after.

BIRTH CONTROL

"Can I get contraceptives?"

This question is being asked by increasing numbers of young people every year. Unfortunately, it has no single answer. The laws in this area are still changing as a result of court battles and decisions by state governments. Depending on where you live, your age, and whether you are married, access to birth control aids may be easy or quite difficult.

Minors who are married have the right to buy contraceptives in every state. This is because the Supreme Court has ruled that it is illegal to prevent married couples from receiving these devices.

Likewise, the Court has said that no one may be denied birth control because they are single. But the question of whether any state may pass a law setting a minimum age when you can get condoms, foams, diaphragms, intrauterine devices (I.U.D.s), or the pill has not yet been answered on a national level. This means that each state can do what it likes.

Today you are able to buy contraceptives on your own in a majority of states. Their number seems to increase every year. Many states have no age requirement at all. Others have set limits that allow virtually everyone to obtain birth control: in California and Oregon a fifteen-year-old can do so without parental consent, and in Alabama you need be only fourteen.

Only a few states still insist on getting permission from your parents until you're over eighteen. Nineteen years of age is the minimum in Nebraska, twenty in Hawaii, and Missouri's is the oldest at twenty-one. But these states are under pressure from the federal government to adopt more liberal laws. In addition, many respected organizations including the American Medical Association support the offering of family planning services and supplies to young people.

How can you find out what your state's policy is? Your doctor can tell you. A phone call or letter to your local Legal Services office or Legal Aid Society will also produce this information. (See list at the end of this book.)

ABORTION

According to a 1978 report by the CBS television network, abortion is now "the hottest controversy going" in the United States. Mass demonstrations by "Pro-Lifers" who oppose abortion and "Reproductive Freedom" advocates who favor it seem to occur weekly in Washington and other major cities. Every politician from the President down to local school board officers is asked to take a stand on the issue. In 1977, anti-abortion groups across the nation spent over a million dollars in their campaign for an amendment to the U.S. Constitution which would prohibit the operation.

In personal terms the question is just as heated and emotional. "An unwanted pregnancy can tear a family apart," says one doctor. "If everyone got together to help the girl it would be one thing. But all too often teen-agers are unable to tell their parents about the problem because they're terrified of being beaten, thrown out of the house, called a whore, or slapped with a statutory rape charge. In some places an unwed mother is treated like a leper. Any of these factors can drive a young person to get an abortion."

Case histories bear him out. One day in 1977, Lisa, a seventeen-year-old high school senior living on Long Island, New York, visited her doctor. When she came out of the office, she knew she was pregnant. "I have to see you right away," she told her boy friend Terry on the phone. In twenty minutes they were driving along the Belt Parkway toward New York City.

Lisa had been struggling to control her feelings since the doctor had told her the test results. But once in the car

87

she broke down. "Terry, I'm pregnant," she sobbed. "I don't want a baby. What are we going to do?"

Jumbled thoughts flashed through Terry's mind. He didn't want to get married. He didn't have the money for an abortion. If his father found out he'd be furious. If *her* folks found out they might have him arrested. Maybe they already knew.

He was confused and panic-stricken. As they drove onto one of the bridges connecting Long Island with the mainland, Terry made a sudden decision. "It's hopeless," he said. "We're better off dead!" With that, he swerved the car into a concrete abutment.

Terry died in the crash. The next day, Lisa went to a local abortion clinic with her leg in a cast. After hearing her story they performed the operation for free.

Four hours later a call came for one of the clinic's counselors. "It's me, Lisa," said an upset voice on the other end. "I'm bleeding. Help me." Fearing that she had been injured by the operation, the counselor raced to her aid. He found her in a phone booth with bruises and a split lip. The reason? When told of the abortion, Lisa's mother had attacked her and told her never to set foot in the house again. It took a week of conferences with clinic workers for Lisa's parents to accept their daughter back home.

Lisa's story is only one of thousands. Obviously, an unwanted pregnancy presents one of the most difficult choices you can make. Religious beliefs and personal needs must be considered and many people seek the advice of close friends, teachers, or relatives. But every year over a million women decide in favor of having an abortion. Many are under eighteen. For them, the main question becomes whether they have a legal right to consent to the operation without an "okay" from their parents.

The 1973 Supreme Court decision that legalized abortions during the first twelve weeks of pregnancy did not mention minors specifically. As a result, many states quickly passed laws requiring minors to get their parents' permission before the operation could take place.

In 1976 the Court struck down those laws. Relying on its earlier ruling that freedom to get an abortion is guaranteed by the U.S. Constitution, the Court wrote: "Constitutional rights do not mature and come into being magically only when one attains the state-defined age of majority. Minors, as well as adults, are protected by the Constitution and possess constitutional rights."

This settled the issue in some states. But others are still trying to limit a young woman's ability to get an abortion on her own. "The latest tactic," says one Pro-Life organizer, "is to pass laws that require proof of parental *knowledge* that the kid is getting aborted, not consent. That way the law is constitutional because, strictly speaking, the decision is still in the hands of the minor. But believe me, if the parents know about the plan to get an abortion and don't want it to happen, it won't."

Another approach has been to require a court hearing when parents won't agree to the operation. A law of this kind was thrown out by a Massachusetts court in 1978, but that hasn't stopped several other states from experimenting with similar regulations.

The result of all this is that a minor must still look to state law to determine what amount of independence she has in getting an abortion. With your parents' consent you can get the operation at any age in any state. Neither a parent nor a legal guardian can legally veto your decision to have a fetus aborted. But some proof of knowledge or consultation with your parents may be necessary in your state.

CHILD-BEARING

Can your parents force you to submit to an abortion if you would rather keep your baby? Although the Supreme Court has not spoken on this issue, the answer is bound to be no. If the constitutional right of privacy allows you the right to choose an abortion, it must stand just as strongly for your right to give birth whether or not you are married. The Constitution protects your right to decide regardless of what decision you make.

Once a child is born, its parents—even if unmarried— take on a whole new legal status. No matter what their age, a mother and father are responsible for the care of their baby. This means they must support the infant. They must supply food and clothing. When the time comes, they must see that the child goes to school.

A teen-age mother also has the power to permit any medical care for herself or the baby. She can even put the child up for adoption if she chooses.

MARRIAGE

Legally, marriage is a contract that is similar in many ways to the business agreements we looked at in Chapter Three. In fact, many state laws explicitly refer to it as a "civil contract."

Like other contracts, marriage confers both rights and duties on husband and wife. In exchange for the right to live together and share property under the law, you are bound to duties such as supporting the family and the care, protection, and education of your children.

What makes marriage different from most contracts is the strict laws that control it. For example, everyone knows that you don't have to go for a medical examination before buying a car. But all states require a doctor's report stating that you are free of venereal disease prior to marriage. Likewise, no state prohibits you from making a contract with your father, (or mother, brother, sister, or uncle or aunt)— unless it's a marriage contract. And while no law prevents young people from buying food, clothing, or books, most states set minimum ages for purchasing a marriage license.

It is this age regulation that concerns most young people today. For those who have decided to set up housekeeping with one of the opposite sex, traditional marriage is still the most popular course. In addition, it is worth remembering that unexpected pregnancy has hastened many couples' plans to tie the knot.

Therefore the question being asked by increasing numbers of teen-agers is, "What are the legal requirements for marriage in my state?"

Most states insist on authorization from a minor's parents or the order of a judge, or both, before they will issue a marriage license. The common rule calls for parental consent if the bride or groom is between sixteen and eighteen years of age, and a court OK on top of that for those under sixteen. This law is enforced in Alaska, Arizona, Colorado, Connecticut, Idaho, Maine, Maryland, Massachusetts, Nevada, New Jersey, New Mexico, Pennsylvania, Tennessee, Vermont and Wyoming.

Several other states apply this rule in modified form. Illinois, North Dakota, Oklahoma, Virginia, Wisconsin and the District of Columbia require consent from your parents between sixteen and eighteen and prohibit marriage under age sixteen.

On the other hand, California, Iowa, Kentucky, Nebraska, Ohio and West Virginia mandate parental consent for all minors under eighteen, but set no rigid minimum age for marriage. Texas is almost as liberal, needing court approval only when the bride or groom is under fourteen.

The remaining twenty-three states have varying requirements:

Alabama demands parental consent and a $200 bond posted with state authorities before anyone under 18 years of age can buy a marriage license.

Minimum ages in *Arkansas* are 17 for boys and 16 for girls, and consent is required if either party is under 18.

Delaware also sets different minimum ages for boys and girls: 18 and 16 respectively. If under 18, the girl must provide written consent from her parents.

Florida requires parental consent unless the bride and groom are over 18 or the one below that age has been married before.

Georgia needs your parents' consent only if you are under 16 years old.

Fifteen is the low age for marriage in *Hawaii*. Between 15 and 16 you need approval from a family court.

Indiana law says that both bride and groom must be over 17 and, if between 17 and 18, have an OK from their parents.

In *Kansas* it is necessary to get approval from your parents and a district court judge if you are under 18.

Louisiana requires parental consent to marry below age 18. If the bride is under 16, a district court must also approve.

Michigan makes 16 the minimum age for girls and 18 the lowest age for boys, with consent of at least one parent mandatory if the bride is under 18.

Minnesota also applies the minimum ages of 16 for girls and 18 for boys. Girls need an OK from their parents and a juvenile court judge if they are between 16 and 18.

Mississippi has set no bottom age for marriage, but boys under 17 and girls under 15 need the consent of their parents and a state court.

Missouri requires parental consent for couples under 18 and an order from circuit or probate court for those under 15.

From age 18 down to 15 in *Montana* you must have authorization to marry from your parents and a district court judge.

New Hampshire law fixes 18 as the minimum marriage age. However, a judge may OK a wedding between a boy as young as 14 and a girl at least 13 years old.

New York's minimum age is 14 for girls, 16 for boys. Written parental consent is required if either party is under 18. The bride must also have a judge's approval if she is under 16.

Young people under 18 in *North Carolina* also need the consent of at least one parent before they get a marriage license. Sixteen is the minimum age for both sexes.

In *Oregon*, kids 17 or older may marry on their own. Under that age parental consent is necessary unless the parents do not reside within the state and either the bride or groom has lived in the county for at least six months.

Rhode Island requires consent from parents and a court if the boy is under 18 or the girl is under 16.

In *South Carolina* parental consent is required from boys from the minimum age of 16 to 18, and girls from the minimum age of 14 to 16.

South Dakota will allow young people between 16 and 18 to marry only if the girl is pregnant or an unwed mother.

Fourteen is the minimum age in *Utah*, with your parents' consent needed if you're under 16.

Washington couples between ages 17 and 18 must get parental consent, and may only marry after getting a court order if they are any younger.

In addition to these age regulations, each state has special rules detailing the form parental consent must take, listing courts that handle marriage requests, and making certain exceptions for pregnant girls and unwed mothers. You can get information on these rules by calling your town or city clerk, court clerk, or local legal aid office.

Thinking of crossing the state line for a quick wedding? Think again. Virtually all states require that you live within their borders for some time before taking advantage of their laws.

VENEREAL DISEASE

Until recently, no one talked much about V.D. It was a "dirty disease." Nice people didn't get it. If you *did* get it you certainly couldn't tell anyone. Maybe, ignorant teenagers sometimes hoped, it would go away quietly like a common cold.

All this silence and embarrassment has made V.D. the most hushed-up epidemic in America. It is estimated that over three million people—more than one percent of our population—are currently afflicted with gonorrhea, syphilis, or some other venereal disease. These infections, if left untreated, will not simply go away but can cause heart problems, nervous system disorders, arthritis, blindness, paralysis, brain damage, or even death. In pregnant women they can cause birth defects or the baby's death.

You don't need your parents' knowledge or permission for a V.D. test or treatment. No matter what your age, public health clinics or private doctors can treat you. There is even a national toll-free telephone number catering specifically to teen-agers who want information about V.D.: (800) 523-1885. This phone is manned by kids your own age who can tell you where to go for a free V.D. exam, or treatment if you already know you have the disease.

PRIVACY

The final point: in every state the relationship between doctor and patient is strictly confidential. This rule spans all ages and all medical procedures. A doctor who is consulted in confidence by a young person has no right to reveal to anyone else—including parents—anything about what went on or what was said. This includes the results of pregnancy tests, V.D. examinations, and abortions. A doctor who violates this rule can be sued for malpractice.

9
Child Abuse and Neglect

Would you help a friend in trouble?

Sure you would. Loyalty in a tough situation is what friendship is all about. For most people this is an informal understanding, though some make it explicit by forming gangs or clubs. On a personal basis, if you have a buddy who is getting beaten up regularly, you come to his aid. If your girl friend is sexually molested, finding the guy who did it gets top priority. If your younger or smaller pal seems to have a fresh black eye, bruise, or welt every time you see him, you find out who is whipping him and even the score.

But would your answer change if the people responsible for your friend's distress are his or her parents?

96

It probably would. Most of us are trained to accept the authority of parents in family matters. We know that many of the rules that govern public life simply don't apply in the home. A mother or father can order their child to work around the house without pay, something that would be laughable if attempted by an employer. Confining a youngster to his or her room would be an offense called "false imprisonment" for anyone but a parent or legal guardian. Laying hands on a stranger is against the law, but the legality of striking a son or daughter is unquestioned. Double standards like these make us reluctant to counsel resistance to parental discipline, however severe.

In most situations, of course, parents try to be firm but kind in correcting their children. Many people regard an occasional spanking or slap as the proper punishment for disobedience. Without doubt, this is a parent's right. But if carried too far, punishment can easily become cruelty. Worse, some adults who suffer from alcoholism, mental illness, or an extremely violent temper may *want* to hurt their kids. When this happens they have exceeded their legal authority. The name of their crime is child abuse, and many social scientists see it as a modern plague.

Child abuse is much more widespread than you might suspect. Between 1967 and 1975 the number of cases reported in the United States rose over 2800 percent. In 1978 it was estimated that between one million and a million and a half American children were physically abused or neglected. In one state alone over forty-two thousand cases were reported in a single year, and undoubtedly there were many more that were never reported.

Experts agree that the problem does not respect economic status. Abused children are as likely to come from comfortable middle-class homes as tenement buildings. Saddest of all, it is also known that the victims of child abuse are prone to continue the cycle by brutalizing their own children years later.

Scary as these statistics are, they do not begin to tell of the suffering and death caused by child abuse. For the human side of the issue, we must look at case histories.

• In California, a mother blinded her five-year-old daughter by smashing an empty glass in her face. The reason: "Jeannie had a sore throat and wouldn't stop whining."

• In New York, a twelve-year-old girl was raped by her father. When his daughter was found to be pregnant the man refused to give permission for an abortion.

• In Michigan, an alcoholic mother tried to drown her four-year-old son while bathing him.

• In Massachusetts, a two-year-old boy was beaten to death by his mother's lover because he wouldn't swallow a doughnut.

Child abuse doesn't exist alone. It has a companion known as child neglect. Child neglect results from one simple fact: it is far easier to make a baby than it is to raise a baby. "Giving birth doesn't carry a dose of instant wisdom," says one social worker. "Every parent has to be taught how to care for a child. In school we spend years learning civics, history, and math, but we don't even mention the responsibilities of parenthood—probably the most important role in anyone's life."

From this incapacity, child neglect is born. In one case a poor woman fed her children almost nothing but ice cream because, she said, "Ice cream is frozen milk and milk is good for babies." The result was malnutrition. In another instance a mother, abandoned by her husband, sank into a deep mental depression and left all the household duties to her five-year-old son. In a short time the house was filthy, infested with cockroaches and empty of food.

These people had no desire to harm their children. The source of their problems was ignorance of nutrition, health, and sanitary conditions. Nonetheless, it was necessary to call in social agencies to assist in working things out.

You and your friends are entitled to proper care while you're dependent on parents or guardians. You also have a right to freedom from abusive treatment. These rules seem simple enough. But, like most other legal rights, they have little meaning without some method of enforcement. This is where child abuse laws have always run into trouble, because every form of "family regulation" has major drawbacks.

The U.S. Constitution guarantees everyone the right of privacy in his or her own home. This means that it would be illegal for police or other government agents to patrol our houses the same way they watch over public streets. Cops must have good reason to suspect that something is wrong before they enter private property. Therefore they can't just "check up" on the way kids are being treated.

Every state requires doctors, dentists, nurses, interns and other hospital personnel to report suspected cases of child abuse. Many states extend this requirement to include public and private school teachers, guidance and family counselors, social workers and policemen. Filing a report of possible abuse or neglect usually sets off an investigation by state welfare workers. If the case turns out to be serious —involving a crime like assault, murder, or rape—legal action may come later.

This sounds like an efficient system. The problem is that it does nothing to prevent child abuse in the first place. A report is made only after the injury is bad enough to put the victim in the hospital or to be noticed by others.

You may be wondering why abused children don't report the situation themselves. On its face, this seems the easiest and most direct method of enforcement. But experience has shown that kids who are brutalized by their parents rarely go to outsiders for help.

The reasons are complex. "They are confused by conflicting emotions," says a psychologist who has worked with many abuse victims. "On one hand there is basic, natural love for their parents. On the other side is a terrific fear of what will happen if dad or mom finds out they went for help. I've seen young people come in with awful bruises or broken bones and say, 'I don't want to get my parents in trouble.' "

Where does this place the task of child abuse prevention? Mostly on the shoulders of young people like yourself. There are several reasons for this. It's logical that the first ones to notice signs of abuse or neglect in a child would be the friends he or she hangs out with every day. If your buddy shows up one morning with an ugly gash on his forehead, you're more apt to notice it than a teacher who looks at hundreds of kids every day or a cop who sees thousands. Because he *is* your buddy you're more likely to ask about the injury than would an official who doesn't know him from Adam.

In addition, young people confide in each other. Your friend would probably tell you things he'd never reveal to an adult. If quizzed about that gash by a teacher or doctor, your pal might say, "It was just an accident—I tripped." But to his friends he will admit, "My old man got mad and threw me against a door last night."

What about other kids on your block or in the neighborhood? They may not speak to you with the frankness of a close friend, but there are other ways to tell when something is amiss. Pamphlets published by your state's Society for the Prevention of Cruelty to Children list many "danger signals" that may indicate child abuse or neglect. These include:

(1) Evidence of repeated bruises or other injuries, especially unusual ones such as cigarette burns and marks left by straps or ropes.

(2) Differences between the degree of injury you observe and the explanation given for it. In one instance a thirteen-year-old girl tried to tell a doctor that her broken arm and huge black eye were the result of walking into a door. The medic was skeptical and later discovered that she had been cruelly beaten for years by her father and stepmother.

(3) Unusually fearful or passive behavior, especially toward parents.

(4) Continual hunger, listlessness, and lack of energy, indicating possible malnutrition.

(5) Inadequate clothing and particularly dirty or unkempt appearance.

(6) Repeated absence from school. (Remember, schooling is compulsory until you're at least fourteen in every state except Mississippi.)

Let's suppose that you have good reason to suspect that your friend is being abused at home. Although things show

101

no sign of getting better, he refuses to seek outside help. Do you have the right to go "over his head" and report the matter anyway?

You do indeed. In fact, anyone with knowledge of this sort of situation has a *duty* to try to get aid. This duty isn't written in law books the way a doctor's or teacher's may be; it should be inscribed on your conscience and motivated by an honest concern for your friend's health and safety. When a young person is being injured or molested it doesn't matter whether the attacker is a parent or a street-corner tough. He or she needs help. Fast.

There is no breach of faith in telling someone about your friend's problem. It isn't "ratting" or "squealing," because child abuse isn't a private matter. If your pal contracted a sickness and no one would care for him you wouldn't hesitate to call in a doctor. You'd notify the police if he were being beaten by hoodlums you couldn't handle on your own. Like sickness and crime, brutality to children is a social problem that should be handled by experts.

Where do you go for help? Generally, your first resort is to the state Department of Public Welfare or Social Services. Frequently these public agencies have 'round-the-clock, toll-free telephone numbers specifically for accepting reports of abuse and neglect. Your state may even have a special government Office for Children, dealing solely with minors' affairs including child abuse.

Just about every state also has a Society for the Prevention of Cruelty to Children. These societies have district offices in most regions which can be called during business hours.

Many organizations will accept an anonymous call reporting suspected abuse or neglect. Some may ask for the caller's name, but this information is rarely revealed to anyone outside the agency.

What happens next? An agency investigator will follow up your phone call with a visit to your friend's home. The investigator will observe conditions in the house and probably speak with the parents. He'll talk with your friend. If he still thinks abuse or neglect may be taking place, he can have the children examined by a physician and can ask questions of the neighbors. His research will continue until he's satisfied that he knows the answer.

The next step depends on what that answer is. If the investigation doesn't indicate improper conditions in the home, the case will be closed. No further action will be taken.

But if the investigator concludes that abuse or neglect is going on, he has many alternatives. His training will enable him to begin trying to figure out what is causing the problem. If the parents show signs of alcoholism or addiction to other drugs he might recommend public treatment programs or private organizations like Alcoholics Anonymous. He can suggest training courses if it appears that the parents don't know how to care for their children. He can refer the family to psychologists, psychiatrists, welfare workers and a host of other government agencies.

If the problem is severe—that is, if your friend's life or health is in immediate danger—the investigator may bypass these general recommendations and advise his bureau to go to court. Lawyers for the government will submit a paper to the judge requesting that he or she officially declare the child "abused" or "neglected." Your friend's parents will be notified of the court hearing before it takes place. They have the right to appear with an attorney of their own to defend their interests. Your friend also has a right to retain his own lawyer at this point.

If the public agency is supposed to be taking the youngster's side, why would he want another counselor? Perhaps the best reason is that state lawyers serve two masters: the child and the government. If the interests of the two come into conflict during the hearing, a dilemma is created.

On the other hand, obtaining a private attorney assures the young person of an advocate who represents him alone. This undivided allegiance may be very important when issues such as placement and care of the abused child are considered. A lawyer may be engaged for this purpose free of charge through a local Legal Aid Society.

If the judge is convinced by all the evidence presented in court that your friend is being abused, he has the power to order various remedies. The most drastic is to remove the young person from home. Where will he go? Some states allow victims of abuse and neglect to stay with a friend or relative. Other places use foster homes for temporary care. In cases where the child shows ill effects from his ordeal, he may be housed in an institution that can give him special treatment.

However, courts are generally reluctant to take children out of their natural homes. A milder solution is for the judge to order your friend's parents to seek professional help and place the situation under observation. This should give your friend protection while allowing the family to work together toward a normal relationship.

Traditionally, child abuse hearings have not been full trials. No one is pronounced guilty or innocent. Parents can't be sent to jail. But today this is changing as states begin to pass laws making child abuse a criminal offense.

In addition, at least one state (Massachusetts) has hastened the crackdown on child abusers by keeping the courts open on weekends and holidays just to handle such cases.

Whether the subject is child abuse, contraception, or contracts, in each case you should be aware that you have a right under the law. Many of these rights have been created within our lifetimes. To ensure their survival, you must fulfill the duties they create—acting responsibly and respecting the freedom of others.

Remember, too, that the civil law can only work for you if you know when to make use of it. Knowing your rights won't guarantee you freedom from legal hassles, but it is your best protection. And it is our legal system that secures your rights.

10
Where to Go for Help

To a young person with a legal problem, the prospect of going to a lawyer for assistance may be almost as frightening as getting arrested. This is because most kids never see lawyers. They imagine attorneys to be severe people who speak a mysterious, technical language and charge a lot of money for everything they do.

This is far from the truth. Lawyers, like doctors, are there to help you out of trouble. An attorney will listen to your story the same way a physician listens to your complaints about aches and pains. Then, after looking into the matter, he or she will either tell you if you can solve the problem on your own or will prescribe a course of action for you to follow.

106

The lawyer may want to speak with your parents—but only if they are involved in the problem or possess some information that can help your case. An obvious example of this is a child abuse situation.

But it's important to remember that an attorney will always respect the privacy of what you have told him. You should not hesitate to tell him if, for any reason, you don't want your parents to be contacted or told certain things. All your discussions will be confidential.

How much will it cost?

Legal aid offices and legal service societies are designed to help young people, poor families, and many others who can't afford to hire a high-priced private lawyer. Their help is frequently free of charge. In some cases they will charge a small fee. Legal aid lawyers realize that cost is a major concern of their clients, so don't be afraid to ask about it at the beginning of your discussion.

How do you find an attorney?

The following list is intended to provide young people with a starting point in solving legal problems. Many of the legal service offices listed here specialize in minors' rights. This is not a complete list of all legal aid offices in the United States, nor of all those that handle young people's problems. But it puts minors in every state a phone call away from legal aid. If any of the organizations listed here can't handle your particular problem, they will refer you to another local office that will help you.

A few special agencies do not appear in the state-by-state listing below. One is the Public Defender's office. Its function is to defend people who get into trouble with the police. You can find a Public Defender's office in every major city.

Another important legal organization is the American Civil Liberties Union. The ACLU is a public-interest body dedicated to upholding the rights of private citizens. The ACLU has a special interest in minorities, including young people. They have legal offices that can aid minors in every state except Idaho, North Dakota, and Wyoming.

Finally, most law schools maintain student-staffed legal assistance offices. These bodies serve members of the local community who cannot afford to hire a private lawyer. Because most of the law students who staff the office are in their twenties, a young person who goes there for aid will find someone who can easily relate to his or her situation.

Appendix

LEGAL AID OFFICES

NATIONAL
National Center for Youth Law
693 Mission Street
San Francisco, California
94105
(415) 543-3307

ACLU Juvenile Rights Project
22 East 40th Street
New York, New York
10016
(212) 725-1222

National Juvenile Law Center
3701 Lindell Boulevard
St. Louis, Missouri
63108
(314) 533-8868

National Legal Aid & Defender
  Assoc.
2100 M Street NW
Washington, D.C.
20037
(202) 452-0620

ALABAMA
Legal Aid Society of Birmingham
2030 First Ave. North
Birmingham, Alabama
35203
(205) 328-3540

Montgomery Legal Services
Alabama Legal Services System
921-A Forest Ave.
Montgomery, Alabama
36106
(205) 264-4333

ALASKA

Alaska Legal Services Corp.
524 West Sixth Ave.
Anchorage, Alaska
99501
(907) 272-9431

—offices also in Fairbanks, Juneau, Sitka and other locations.

ARIZONA

Maricopa County Legal Aid
 Society
903 North Second Street
Phoenix, Arizona
85040
(602) 258-3434

Pima County Legal Aid Society
55 West Congress Street
Tucson, Arizona
85701
(602) 623-6260

ARKANSAS

Legal Aid Bureau of Pulaski
 County
1520 Broadway
Little Rock, Arkansas
72202
(501) 376-3423

Jackson County Legal Services
P.O. Box 623
Newport, Arkansas
72112
(501) 523-2312

CALIFORNIA

Legal Aid Foundation of Los
 Angeles
1819 West Sixth Street
Los Angeles, California
90057
(213) 484-9550

Legal Aid Society of Alameda
 County
1815 Telegraph Ave.
Oakland, California
94612
(415) 451-9261

Merced Legal Services
1812 L Street
P.O. Box 1310
Merced, California
95340
(209) 723-5466

Legal Aid Society of San Diego
400 Granger Building; 964 Fifth
 Ave.
San Diego, California
92101
(714) 239-9611

COLORADO

Colorado Rural Legal Services
626 Main Street
P.O. Box 569
Alamosa, Colorado
81101
(303) 589-4993

Legal Aid Society of Metropolitan
Denver
912 Broadway
Denver, Colorado
80203
(303) 837-1313

CONNECTICUT
Neighborhood Legal Services,
Inc.
9 Center Street
Hartford, Connecticut
06120
(203) 547-1990

New Haven Legal Assistance
265 Church Street
New Haven, Connecticut
06511
(203) 777-7601

—also Connecticut Legal Services offices in Bridgeport, Danbury, Middletown and other locations.

DELAWARE
Community Legal Aid Society
18 South Race Street
Georgetown, Delaware
19947
(302) 856-0038

FLORIDA
Duval County Legal Aid Assoc.
205 East Church Street
Jacksonville, Florida
32202
(904) 356-8375

Legal Services of Greater Miami
1393 Southwest First Street
Miami, Florida
33135
(305) 579-5757

Law, Inc. of Hillsborough County
1155 East Cass Street
Tampa, Florida
33602
(813) 223-2525

GEORGIA
Atlanta Legal Aid Society
153 Pryor Street Southwest
Atlanta, Georgia
30303
(404) 524-8807

—also has offices in Decatur, Lawrenceville, and Marietta.

HAWAII
Legal Aid Society of Hawaii
1164 Bishop Street (Main Office)
Honolulu, Hawaii
96813
(808) 536-4302

—also has offices in Hilo, Kona, Wailuku and other locations.

IDAHO
Lewis-Clark Legal Services
P.O. Box 573
Lewiston, Idaho
83501
(208) 743-1156

—also Idaho Legal Services offices in Boise, Caldwell, Idaho Falls, Twin Falls and other locations.

ILLINOIS

Juvenile Court Legal Services—
United Charities of Chicago
1114 South Oakley Boulevard
Chicago, Illinois
60612
(312) 421-2061

Land of Lincoln Legal Assistance
Foundation
234 Collinsville Ave.
East St. Louis, Illinois
62201
(618) 271-9140

—also in Cairo, Champaign, Madison,
Mt. Vernon and other locations.

Cook County Legal Assistance
Foundation
828 Davis Street
Evanston, Illinois
60201
(312) 475-3703

INDIANA

Legal Services
402 East Main Street
Fort Wayne, Indiana
46802
(219) 743-7351

Legal Services—Legal Education
Program
204 South William Street
South Bend, Indiana
46625
(219) 287-1056

Legal Services Organization of
Indiana, Inc.
107 North Pennsylvania Street
Indianapolis, Indiana
46204
(317) 639-4151

IOWA

Legal Aid Society of Polk County
102 East Grand Ave.
Des Moines, Iowa
50309
(515) 243-1193

Hawkeye Area Legal Services
Society
255 South Gilbert Street
Iowa City, Iowa
52240
(319) 351-6570

KANSAS

Wyandotte County Legal Aid
Society
907 North Seventh Street
Kansas City, Kansas
66101
(913) 621-0200

Legal Aid Society of Wichita
104 South Broadway
Wichita, Kansas
67202
(316) 265-9681

Legal Aid Society of Topeka
121 East Sixth Street
Topeka, Kansas
66603
(913) 354-8531

KENTUCKY
Kentucky Child Advocacy
  Council
710 West High Street
Lexington, Kentucky
40508
(606) 254-3431

Legal Aid Society
422 West Liberty Street
Louisville, Kentucky
40202
(502) 584-1254

LOUISIANA
Southwest Louisiana Legal
  Services
2225 Moeling Street
P.O. Box 3002
Lake Charles, Louisiana
70601
(318) 436-3308

New Orleans Legal Assistance
  Corp.
226 Carondelet Street
New Orleans, Louisiana
70130
(504) 529-7551

MAINE
Pine Tree Legal Assistance
Coe Building, Room 53
61 Main Street
Bangor, Maine
04401
(207) 942-8241
—also has offices in Lewiston, Augusta, and other locations including Portland, at 146 Middle Street. (207) 774-8211

MARYLAND
Legal Aid Bureau, Inc., at several locations in Baltimore and other offices in Annapolis, Bel Air, Hughsville, and Mt. Rainier.

MASSACHUSETTS
Greater Boston Legal Services
14 Somerset Street
Boston, Massachusetts
02108
(617) 227-0200

Legal Services for Cape Cod &
  Islands
138 Winter Street
Hyannis, Massachusetts
02601
(617) 775-7020

Western Massachusetts Legal
  Services
121 Chestnut Street
Springfield, Masachusetts
01103
(413) 781-7814

Cambridge & Somerville Legal
Services
24 Thorndyke Street
East Cambridge, Massachusetts
02139
(617) 492-5520

Neighborhood Legal Services
31 Exchange Street
Lynn, Massachusetts
01901
(617) 599-7730

MICHIGAN
Washtenaw County Legal Aid
Society
212 East Huron Street
Ann Arbor, Michigan
48108
(313) 665-6181

Legal Aid & Defender's Assoc.
of Kent Co.
1208 McKay Tower
Grand Rapids, Michigan
49502
(616) 451-2504

Legal Aid & Defender Assoc.
of Detroit
51 West Warren Ave.
Detroit, Michigan
48201
(313) 833-2980

Greater Lansing Legal Aid
Bureau
300 North Washington Ave.
P.O. Box 1071
Lansing, Michigan
48906
(517) 484-7773

MINNESOTA
Legal Aid Society of Minneapolis
501 Park Ave.
Minneapolis, Minnesota
55415
(612) 332-1441

Southern Minnesota Regional
Legal Services
370 Selby Ave.
St. Paul, Minnesota
55102
(612) 222-5863

MISSISSIPPI
Jackson-Hinds Community Legal
Services
107 Farish Street
P.O. Box 22571
Jackson, Mississippi
39205
(601) 355-0671

MISSOURI
Juvenile Defense Unit—
Legal Aid
2535 Charlotte Street
Kansas City, Missouri
64106
(816) 421-2141

Legal Air & Defender Society of
Greater Kansas City
1029 Oak Street
Kansas City, Missouri
64106
(816) 474-6750

—also has offices in Independence and
Platte City.

MONTANA
Missoula-Mineral County Legal
Services
127 East Main Street
Missoula, Montana
59801
(406) 543-8343

Montana Legal Services Associa-
tion offices in Billings, Butte,
Glendive, Lewistown, Wolf
Point and other locations.

NEBRASKA
Legal Aid Society of Omaha-
Council Bluffs, Inc.
1613 Farnam Street
Omaha, Nebraska
68102
(402) 348-1060

NEVADA
Clark County Public Defender
309 South Third Street
Las Vegas, Nevada
89101
(702) 386-4011

NEW HAMPSHIRE
New Hampshire Legal Assistance
88 Hanover Street
Manchester, New Hampshire
03101
(603) 668-2900

—also has offices in Berlin, Concord,
Keene, Lebanon, Nashua and other
locations.

NEW JERSEY
Cape-Atlantic Legal Services
1516 Atlantic Ave.
Atlantic City, New Jersey
08401
(609) 348-4200

—also has offices in Cape May, Villas
and Wildwood.

Essex-Newark Legal Services
Project
463 Central Ave.
Newark, New Jersey
07107
(201) 485-3800

Hudson County Legal Services
Corp.
628 Newark Ave.
Jersey City, New Jersey
07306
(201) 792-6363

—also has an office in Union City.

Passaic County Legal Aid Society
140 Market Street
Paterson, New Jersey
07505
(201) 525-4068

115

NEW MEXICO
Legal Aid Society of Albuquerque, Inc.
505 Marquette, Northwest
P.O. Box 7538
Albuquerque, New Mexico
87104
(505) 243-7871

Sante Fe Legal Aid Society
322 Montezuma Ave.
Santa Fe, New Mexico
87501
(505) 982-9886

NEW YORK
Broome Legal Assistance Corp.
30 Fayette Street
Binghamton, New York
13901
(607) 723-7966

Legal Aid Society, Family Court
Branch
283 Adams Street
Brooklyn, New York
11201
(212) 855-8473

Nassau County Law Services
285 Fulton Ave.
Hempstead, New York
11550
(516) 538-3121
—also has offices in Freeport, Glen
Cove and other towns.

Legal Aid Society
1029 East 163rd Street
Bronx, New York
10459
(212) 991-4600

Legal Aid Bureau of Buffalo
Walbridge Building
Buffalo, New York
14202
(716) 853-9555

Community Action for Legal
Services
335 Broadway
New York, New York
10013
(212) 966-6600

Harlem Assertion of Rights, Inc.
35-43 West 125th Street
New York, New York
10029
(212) 586-4270

Legal Aid Society
2011 Mott Ave.
Far Rockaway, New York
11691
(212) 337-4900

Mobilization for Youth Legal
Services
214 East Second Street
New York, New York
10009
(212) 777-5250

116

Legal Aid Society of Oneida
County
239 Genesee Street
Utica, New York
13501
(315) 732-2131

NORTH CAROLINA
Legal Aid Society of Mecklen-
burg County
403 North Tryon Street
Charlotte, North Carolina
28202
(704) 376-1608

Legal Aid Society of Wake
County
127 West Hargett Street
Raleigh, North Carolina
27601
(919) 828-4647

NORTH DAKOTA
North Dakota Legal Services
P.O. Box 4
New Town, North Dakota
58763
(701) 627-4719

Legal Assistance of North Dakota
420 North Fourth Street
Bismarck, North Dakota
58501
(701) 258-4270

OHIO
Legal Aid Society of Cleveland
1223 West Sixth Street
Cleveland, Ohio
44113
(216) 687-1900

Legal Aid Society of Cincinnati
2400 Reading Road
Cincinnati, Ohio
45202
(513) 241-9400

Ohio State Legal Services Asoc.
8 East Broad Street
Columbus, Ohio
43215
(614) 221-2668

Toledo Legal Aid Society
1 Stranahan Square
Toledo, Ohio
43604
(419) 244-9585

OKLAHOMA
Tulsa County Legal Aid Society,
Inc.
Center Building, 630 West
Seventh Street
Tulsa, Oklahoma
74127
(918) 584-3338

OREGON
Legal Aid Service
310 Southwest Fourth Street
Portland, Oregon
97204
(503) 224-4086

PENNSYLVANIA
Lehigh Valley Legal Services
133 North Fifth Street
Allentown, Pennsylvania
18102
(215) 821-8545
—also has offices in Bethlehem and Easton.

Legal Services, Inc.
110 South Washington Street
Gettysburg, Pennsylvania
17325
(717) 334-7623

Community Legal Services
Juniper & Locust Streets
Philadelphia, Pennsylvania
19107
(215) 893-5300

Central Pennsylvania Legal
  Services
524 Washington Street
Reading, Pennsylvania
19601
(215) 376-8656

Delaware County Legal
  Assistance Assoc.
410 Welsh Street
Chester, Pennsylvania
19013
(215) 874-8421

Tri-County Legal Services
48 North Duke Street
Lancaster, Pennsylvania
17602
(717) 299-0971

Neighborhood Legal Services
  Assoc.
535 Fifth Ave.
Pittsburgh, Pennsylvania
15219
(412) 281-1662

RHODE ISLAND
Rhode Island Legal Services
58 Pine Street
Providence, Rhode Island
02903
(401) 331-4665

SOUTH CAROLINA
Neighborhood Legal Assistance
  Program
119 Spring Street
Charleston, South Carolina
29403
(803) 722-0107

Legal Aid Service Agency
1316 Main Street
P.O. Box 1056
Columbia, South Carolina
29202
(803) 779-9668

Legal Services Agency of
  Greenville County
South Carolina National Bank
  Building
13 South Main Street
Greenville, South Carolina
29601
(803) 233-2779

SOUTH DAKOTA
South Dakota Legal Services
  offices in Batesland, Eagle
  Butte, Ft. Thompson, Mission
  and Wagner.

TENNESSEE
Southeast Tennessee Legal
  Services
540 McCallie Ave.
Chattanooga, Tennessee
37402
(615) 266-8188

Legal Services of Nashville &
  Middle Tennessee
1512 Parkway Towers
Nashville, Tennessee
37219
(615) 244-6610

Memphis & Shelby County
  Legal Services
325 Dermon Building
46 North Third Street
Memphis, Tennessee
38103
(901) 526-5132

TEXAS
Legal Aid & Defender Society
  of Travis County
P.O. Box 2213
Austin, Texas
78767
(512) 474-1531

El Paso Legal Assistance
109 North Oregon Street
El Paso, Texas
79901
(915) 544-3022

Houston Legal Foundation
609 Fanin Building
Houston, Texas
77002
(713) 225-0321

Dallas Legal Aid Society
502 States General Life Building
708 Jackson Street
Dallas, Texas
75202
(214) 742-7650

UTAH
Salt Lake County Bar Legal
 Services
216 East Fifth South Street
Salt Lake City, Utah
84111
(801) 328-8891

VERMONT
Vermont Legal Aid offices in
 Bennington, Brattleboro, Bur-
 lington, Montpelier, Rutland
 and other locations.

VIRGINIA
Alexandria Legal Aid Society
815 King Street
Alexandria, Virginia
22314
(703) 750-6438

Tidewater Legal Aid Society
712 Duke Street
Norfolk, Virginia
23510
(703) 625-7079

Legal Aid Society of Roanoke
 Valley
312 Church Ave. Southwest
Roanoke, Virginia
24016
(703) 344-2088

Charlottesville-Albemarle Legal
 Aid Society
420 Third Street Northeast
Charlottesville, Virginia
22901
(804) 293-5131
Metropolitan Richmond Legal
 Aid Project
18 North Eighth Street
Richmond, Virginia
23219
(703) 648-2821

WASHINGTON
Evergreen Legal Services offices
 in Clarkson, Everett, Seattle
 and other locations.

Pierce County Legal Assistance
 Foundation
744 Market Street
Tacoma, Washington
98402
(206) 572-4343

WEST VIRGINIA
Appalachian Research & Defense
 Fund
11168 Kanawha Boulevard East
Charleston, West Virginia
25301
(304) 344-9687

North Central West Virginia
 Legal Aid Society
446 Spruce Street
Morgantown, West Virginia
26505
(304) 296-3100

WISCONSIN
Legal Services Center
122 South Pinckney Ave.
Madison, Wisconsin
53703
(608) 262-0626

WYOMING
Legal Aid Services, Inc.
202 Con Roy Building
Casper, Wyoming
82601
(307) 235-2786

LEGAL ASSISTANCE OFFICES AT LAW SCHOOLS

University of Alabama
Tuscaloosa, Alabama
35401

Cumberland Law School
Birmingham, Alabama
35209

University of California
Los Angeles, California
90024

Hastings College of Law
San Francisco, California
94102

McGeorge College of Law
Sacramento, California
95817

University of San Diego
San Diego, California
92110

University of Santa Clara
Santa Clara, California
95053

Stanford University
Stanford, California
94305

University of Colorado
Boulder, Colorado
80302

University of Denver
Denver, Colorado
80210

University of Connecticut
Storrs, Connecticut
06268

Yale University
New Haven, Connecticut
06520

Georgetown University
Washington, D.C.
20001

Howard University
Washington, D.C.
20001

University of Miami
Coral Gables, Florida
33124

Stetson University
DeLand, Florida
32720

121

University of Georgia
Athens, Georgia
30601

University of Kentucky
Lexington, Kentucky
40506

Emory University
Atlanta, Georgia
30601

University of Louisville
Louisville, Kentucky
40208

University of Chicago
Chicago, Illinois
60637

Tulane University
New Orleans, Louisiana
70118

Northwestern University
Chicago, Illinois
60611

University of Maryland
Baltimore, Maryland
21201

University of Illinois
Urbana, Illinois
61820

Boston College
Newton Centre, Massachusetts
02159

University of Indiana
Indianapolis, Indiana
46204

Harvard University
Cambridge, Massachusetts
02138

University of Notre Dame
Notre Dame, Indiana
46556

University of Detroit
Detroit, Michigan
48221

Drake University
Des Moines, Iowa
50311

University of Michigan
Ann Arbor, Michigan
48104

University of Kansas
Lawrence, Kansas
66044

University of Minnesota
Minneapolis, Minnesota
55455

Washburn University
Topeka, Kansas
66621

University of Missouri
Kansas City, Missouri
64110

Washington University
St. Louis, Missouri
63130

Syracuse University
Syracuse, New York
13210

University of Nebraska
Lincoln, Nebraska
68508

University of North Carolina
Chapel Hill, North Carolina
27515

Rutgers University
New Brunswick, New Jersey
08903

University of North Dakota
Grand Forks, North Dakota
58201

Seton Hall University
South Orange, New Jersey
07079

Akron University
Akron, Ohio
44304

University of New Mexico
Albuquerque, New Mexico
87106

University of Cincinnati
Cincinnati, Ohio
45219

Brooklyn Law School
Brooklyn, New York
11201

Ohio Northern University
Ada, Ohio
45810

University of Buffalo
Buffalo, New York
14214

Ohio State University
Columbus, Ohio
43210

Columbia Univeristy
New York, New York
10027

University of Toledo
Toledo, Ohio
43606

Cornell University
Ithaca, New York
14850

Western Reserve University
Cleveland, Ohio
44106

State University of New York
Albany, New York
12203

University of Oklahoma
Norman, Oklahoma
73069

University of Tulsa
Tulsa, Oklahoma
74103

University of Texas
Austin, Texas
78705

University of Oregon
Eugene, Oregon
97403

Texas Southern University
Houston, Texas
77004

Dickinson Law School
Carlisle, Pennsylvania
17013

University of Utah
Salt Lake City, Utah
84112

University of Pittsburgh
Pittsburgh, Pennsylvania
15213

University of Richmond
Richmond, Virginia
23173

Temple University
Philadelphia, Pennsylvania
19122

University of Virginia
Charlottesville, Virginia
22901

Villanova University
Villanova, Pennsylvania
19085

Washington & Lee University
Lexington, Virginia
24450

University of South Dakota
Vermillion, South Dakota
57069

College of William and Mary
Williamsburg, Virginia
23185

University of Tennessee
Knoxville, Tennessee
37916

Gonzaga University
Spokane, Washington
99202

Baylor University
Waco, Texas
76703

University of Washington
Seattle, Washington
98105

Southern Methodist University
Dallas, Texas
75222

West Virginia University
Morgantown, West Virginia
26505

Marquette University
Milwaukee, Wisconsin
53233

University of Wisconsin
Madison, Wisconsin
53706

University of Wyoming
Laramie, Wyoming
82070

Index